The moment you become a father, *you find yourself making some big promises. It doesn't matter that ten minutes ago you hyperventilated into a paper bag while your wife endured childbirth. Or that the labor nurse had to offer you a "little something" for your nerves. As you cradle that baby for the first time, you just can't stop yourself. In an adrenaline rush, you silently swear to be a paragon of virtue, to be strong, kind, brave, prudent, smart about money, and good with tools. In short, you promise to be somebody else. Somebody better.*

I remember my promises to our son, Josh. I would be the source of laughter, comfort, peanut butter, stories, faith, hope, and training wheels. I would make sure the snow tires were on the car before the first blizzard. I would be his hero.

I kept all my promises . . . until we took him home from the hospital. That's when my big, swaggering Daddy dreams started to come apart at the seams.

I got bushwhacked by fatherhood. I had no idea what was ahead of me, no idea what I was about to go through.

I had no idea that I would one day reach into the glove box for a map and get bitten by a turtle. Or that I would ever swallow a little green Monopoly house. I never imagined I would learn the gestation period of domestic hamsters. Or find fruit in my shoes. I had no idea that Josh and his sister, Rebecca—who was to follow three years later—would call my bluff on every blowhard promise I had ever made. Of course, I also had no idea I could feel so deeply, or that tucking children in would have the serenity of prayer, or that being their father would renovate my heart.

Only now—after a decade of Daddy tumult, delight, and dread—can I see clearly. Now I know that fatherhood is a bridge, a passage from all those windy, heroic vows to the real-life elations of doing your best on behalf of the kids. Now I know that fatherhood is a pilgrim's path, littered with marbles and most of your plans.

My wisdom didn't come easy. I had to survive the minigolf disaster at the Poconos Putt-o-Rama and that incident with the circus clown. I had to rescue Mr. Buttons from the median strip of I-95. I had to spend a little over a zillion dollars on batteries.

I had to take a fall before I saw the light.

Also by Hugh O'Neill

Daddy Cool
Here's Looking at You, Kids

Hugh O'Neill

RUTLEDGE HILL PRESS™

Nashville, Tennessee

A Division of Thomas Nelson, Inc.
www.ThomasNelson.com

Published by Rutledge Hill Press, Inc., a Division of Thomas Nelson, Inc., P.O. Box 141000, Nashville, Tennessee 37214.

Typography by E. T. Lowe, Nashville, Tennessee.

Library of Congress Cataloging-in-Publication Data

O'Neill, Hugh.
    A man called Daddy / Hugh O'Neill.
        p.   cm.
    ISBN 1-55853-997-2
    1. Fatherhood—Humor.   2. Fathers—Humor.   I. Title.
PN6231.F37056   1996
818'.5403—dc20

                                                            95-26787
                                                            CIP

Printed in the United States of America

02 03 04 05 06—9 8 7 6 5 4 3 2 1

TO

Josh and Rebecca,
with thanks
for the pleasure of your
company

Contents

Daddy Takes the Fall

OR

Of High Noon and Hey, Dad

Until The Night of My Great Fall, I had always enjoyed my nightly lock-up rounds. With Jody and the kids asleep upstairs, I would cruise through the house, a sentry in his underwear, turning off the lights, checking the doors, indulging myself in lord-of-the-manor thoughts. I took an unseemly pride in pulling up the drawbridge to our fortress.

Often as I bent to pick up a deserted yo-yo or sneaker, I had dark, out-of-nowhere thoughts about how I would pulverize any intruder into Castle O'Neill. No matter that I am a man of modest strength. In my Daddy fantasies, I had studied kickboxing. I was devastating in defense of the home ground. The coroner would only be able to speculate as to the cause of the bad guy's death: "Massive trauma from a super-human, probably paternal, force."

The truth is that some corner of my Daddy heart looked forward to a confrontation, actually wanted a chance to prove myself, to summon my muscle and will on behalf of my team. No doubt my dreams of protective mayhem were cover for my day-to-day failings. Sure, I might sometimes be too tired to listen to Josh's jokes or help Rebecca with her homework. But in a real crisis, I told myself, Daddy would ride to the rescue.

The Night of the Great Fall, however, all those fierce notions of fatherhood went head-over-heels.

At the top of the stairs, my foot hooked Rebecca's Baby Sweet doll carriage, also known as a booby trap planted by fate. I stumbled, grabbed for the banister, and missed. As I began to plunge, in free fall, down the stairs, I was sure of only one thing: I'd need medical attention on impact. I remember the squawk of the doll *in* the carriage. "Hi, my name is Sparkle," her computer-chip voice said.

I hit the stairs with a thud, bounced off the wall, and kaboomed downward, the doll carriage wrapped around my foot like an oversized ankle bracelet. As I crashed hard in the foyer, Sparkle went flying into the front door.

"Let's take a walk," she said. "I like to take walks."

Splayed out on the floor, I moaned. Then I got to my hands and knees and tried to stand up. But my right

14

ankle wouldn't take the weight. I crumpled back to the floor, knocking over Sparkle on the way.

"Do you love me?" she said.

"Give it a rest, doll," I muttered, in no mood for chitchat.

Even in my wounded state, I didn't forget my duties. As I stretched up to turn the lock on the front door, I suddenly pictured myself now helpless against the same hypothetical intruder I had pole-axed just a minute before. First, I imagined myself reduced to speaking sternly to him: "Hey, buster, this is private property." Then I imagined a different coroner's report: "O'Neill died of shame that he couldn't protect his family."

Helpless on the floor, I had a snake's-eye view of the house. Over to my right, on the floor in the living room, were a half-eaten cookie, a Dr. Seuss book, a soccer ball, a small sock, and Barbie's plastic friend, Midge—who was wearing only a single golden high-heel. Under the phone table was a plastic wizard sword. I reached out and took up the blade. And as I actually wondered if I could use it against the imaginary intruder, I started laughing. In that ridiculous moment—as I brandished a polypropylene sword at a nonexistent trespasser—I saw through all those heroic delivery room promises.

Somehow the sight of all those sweet, silly artifacts of family life scattered around the room made everything clear to me. The enemy isn't *out there*. The enemy is already *inside* the house. The enemy isn't some crook in a ski mask. No, the enemy is fatigue and carelessness and all our cherished dumb ideas. The question isn't how many threats you can repel from *out there*, but how much affection you can summon from *inside* your heart.

Inspired by my newfound wisdom, I somehow got up and hobbled through my night-watchman rounds. Still carrying my plastic Excalibur, I crawled upstairs into Rebecca's room and, for a moment, just watched my daughter sleep, savoring the huffing of the child at rest. Gazing at her, I knew, suddenly and certainly, that fatherhood isn't puffed up with promises. I knew that Dad isn't tested in a shootout on Main Street but in dozens of modest daily moments of shoe-tying and cheerleading. Fatherhood is a thousand small acts of stewardship and hope, steadfastness and care.

As I climbed into bed next to Jody, I riffled through my mental file of father failures: all the times I went ballistic over inconsequential crimes; all the times I managed to say just the *wrong* thing to the kids. Lying there next to my partner, I couldn't help wondering if I had enough father stuff inside me—enough goodness, enough patience, enough energy, enough facts about the Civil War—to give the kids access to the human hymn. As I fell asleep, I resolved to make fewer promises and pay more attention.

I still have a souvenir of The Night of the Great Fall. Every now and then I'll be walking along, step on a small stone or crack in the pavement, and I'll feel my ankle start to twist. Sometimes I'll even fall, just the way I went down that night. But more often, my trick ankle is only a twinge, a sharp anatomical reminder of the two irrefutable fatherhood facts.

First, fatherhood is a chance to fall down the stairs, to be clumsy and careless, to let children down every day in every way. But second, and far more encouraging, fatherhood is also a forum for the best we've got, a chance to be fair and funny and noble and good, a chance to matter, a chance to be both humble and proud, to feed the hungry, comfort the weary, rally the faint of heart, and pitch to the very small.

Fatherhood is the chance we've been waiting for.

Daddy at Sea

OR

Pedaling, Pedaling over the Bounding Main

Everybody knows about the physical demands of motherhood. Mothers, quite rightly, earn sympathy for surviving morning sickness, weight gain, the storm of labor itself. But with all due respect for the nine-month ordeal, the plain truth is that once the baby's a year old, it's Dad who puts on the harness.

It's Dad who carries the kids to the car, Dad who rides the roller coasters, Dad who assembles the jungle gym, Dad who does piggyback duty. Sure, pregnancy is no picnic. But try having somewhere between twenty-eight and sixty-six pounds hanging around your neck for six, seven, eight years. It makes the last trimester feel like an afternoon nap. Fatherhood is the ironman triathlon.

More important, the physical trials of fatherhood usually come out of nowhere. One minute, you're walking happily along licking an ice-cream cone, the next, you're in the middle of a cardiopulmonary emergency, sucking wind, doubled over in oxygen-debt, gasping for air.

JODY AND I had collaborated on a perfect Baltimore day for our team. We had visited the world-class aquarium, prowled through an old submarine and across a three-masted schooner in the harbor. We had bought everything edible from crab cakes to Rocky Road ice cream, everything wearable from T-shirts to whale hats. We had even bought a cassette of songs about plankton. The cool March day was drifting toward dusk when Josh and Rebecca hit us with the demand we had dreaded from the moment we had arrived.

"Oh, Daddy, can we ride the paddleboats? Please, Daddy, please. They're the best," the kids said in sync.

Our options were clear. We could trash all the good memories we'd banked over the previous six hours, or we could head out to sea—like the dozens of other families who flecked the harbor—on one of those plastic pontoons with pedals. Jody and I looked at each other through desperate eyes.

"Doesn't it feel a little cold to you?" she asked, looking for an escape route.

But there was nowhere to hide. Anchors aweigh, my boys.

"That'll be $12.50, plus a $5 deposit on the boat," said a sailor-capped teenage girl behind the counter. "Be back by 5:22," she went on, looking at a giant clock on the dock, "or we charge you for another half-hour." I'm sure what she meant to say was, "Fair breeze to you, sailor."

"Aye, aye, sir," I replied, the most cheerful man in America, "back in the slip by 5:22." My nautical spit-and-polish went unnoticed.

We walked down the gangplank to the dock where a seventeen-year-old harbormaster in a torn T-shirt tossed us some life jackets and gave us a quick navigation lesson. "Forward to go left," he said, pointing to a stick shift amidships, "backward to go right."

"Don't you mean 'port' and 'starboard,' captain?" I asked, merrily. He looked at me blankly.

"Your half-hour's up at 5:22," he said, pointing to the giant clock, shoving us away from the dock with his foot and nearly sending Rebecca over the side. "Be back or we keep your deposit."

Now, the notion that somebody would make off with one of these "boats"—and I use the word as sarcastically as possible—ranked right up there with the preposterous ideas of our time. This was a fifteen-foot-long, molded-plastic, pontooned monstrosity.

Unrelated to any other seagoing vessel, it was half-bathtub/half-Schwinn, designed to be pedaled through the ocean white with foam. Believe me, anybody off-kilter enough to even think about stealing one of these boats wouldn't give the five-buck deposit a second thought. In fact, he'd probably struggle with the whole concept of legal tender.

This was not exactly the seagoing scene of my dreams. This was not the children scampering over the deck, tying lines to cleats, aglow in the blue-sky life Jody and I had made for them in Hyannis. No, I was bent forward at the waist, pedaling a plastic barge. Not exactly swashbuckling. This wasn't Kennedyesque; this was positively Nixonian.

Still, for the first few minutes our "voyage" was smooth. I laid manfully into the pedals. The kids burbled away. Rebecca asked if we could get to Alaska by going that way, Daddy. The kids loved being out on the water—the perfect climax to a perfect day with their perfect parents. Jody, her hair afire with the Maryland dusk, looked at me as though this was the life she'd imagined.

But I knew something Jody and the kids didn't know. I knew that this was the most inefficient craft ever devised. I knew that to move us ten yards through perfectly placid water demanded an energy output that could have powered the village of East

McKeesport, Pennsylvania, for five weeks. Most important, I knew that, though my legs were still furiously pedaling the USS *God Help Me*, I had absolutely no sensation from my hipbones to my toes.

Jody turned to me and caught my expression. "Are you all right, Hugh?" she inquired.

Though I couldn't actually speak, I tried to reassure her with a carefree little "I'm cool" wave. I knew enough about biomechanics to know that the paralysis in my southern half was nothing more serious than the buildup of lactose in my leg muscles, each of which had just fired over four million times in a span of twelve minutes.

The hair on my legs felt like it was going to ignite.

"Hugh, I'd feel better if you'd say something," she said, now rather more nervous than before.

I waved reassuringly again.

"What's that guy's name at Prudential?" she asked, as though she was sorry to cut to the life-insurance chase, but she had the children to think of.

As she was mentally preparing herself for widowhood and I was pondering the sweet brevity of our passage through this vale of tears, Josh said, "Daddy, why can't we go out as far as everybody else?"

He was pointing to a small paddleboat speck out in the shipping lanes, some errant paternal pedaler who was either committing Viking suicide or else didn't give a damn about his deposit. Otherwise, we were, I swear, farther out than every other boat. But as always with kids, they didn't notice what we had given them, only what we hadn't.

Then the wind began to pick up a bit and the water began to chop. Suddenly the sky grew dark and the temperature dropped dramatically. I looked around and saw all the Dads leaning on the stick shifts, trying to come about and head for safe harbor.

The invasion at Normandy, this wasn't. No. This was a squeamish armada. Forty-two red-faced fathers doubled over amidships, madly pedaling into the wind, racing both the coming squall and the giant taunting clock that threatened them with an additional charge of $12.50.

It was 5:17, T minus five minutes.

When I realized that the wind would make the voyage home twice as hard as the outward leg, I panicked. I thought about simply heading out to sea and hanging a right toward Charleston. Make a run for it, I thought. That'd show 'em. What did these guys think? I couldn't blow off the five-buck deposit? "Keep the five spot, suckers," I muttered as I considered my options. "I've got your bathtub."

It was 5:18, T-minus four minutes.

"Dad, you've only got four minutes," Josh said, as though we were racing against a detonator and not some arbitrary deadline imposed by a kid whose complexion wasn't his strong suit.

Still, for some reason, it was important to me that we get back by 5:22. Not because of the money. The only way they'd squeeze another $12.50 out of this sailor was for a court to attach my salary. Indeed, as the clock moved to 5:21, I wondered if I could interest the other Daddies in a class-action suit against the city, the mayor, and the kid in the T-shirt.

Anyway, we didn't make it. As the clock turned to 5:23, Rebecca said, "Uh-oh, Daddy," as though I were just going to have to be a little more responsible.

When we finally got back to the dock and I tried to climb off the "boat," I nearly fell into the harbor, soaking my left leg up to my crotch. My deck shoe sank full fathom five. As I pulled myself up on the dock, I stumbled and took a splinter in my knee.

The clock read 5:25.

The teenage harbormaster looked as though he were about to say something about an additional charge. "Don't even think about it," I said. All around me, men were climbing out of boats, wobbling onto the dock. One father in a ball cap collapsed onto all fours. Another was leaning on his three-year-old.

I galoomphed, shoeless and annoyed, toward the car. One mother, pushing a stroller of twins, gave me a wide berth.

Standing in the parking lot, I took off my soaked pants and slipped behind the wheel, wearing boxer shorts and one shoe. The next thing I remember is Jody covering me with a blanket as we pulled into a toll-booth just south of Philly.

"Everything all right, ma'am?" the tollbooth guy asked, peering past me to Jody, as though his fine-tuned criminal radar had picked up the vibe "hostage drama."

"Daddy took off his pants," Becky answered help-fully.

"It's a misdemeanor to drive without shoes, sir," he said, sneaking a peak toward my lap.

With that I floored it and fish-tailed out of there.

"Is Daddy going to prison, Mommy?" Becky asked.

"I get the front seat if he does," Josh chimed in.

It had come to this. Driving half-naked with one shoe, getting a lecture from a toll taker, and enduring a son who saw Dad doing eighteen months upstate as a chance to trade up, seating-wise.

"Nobody's going to jail," Jody said as matter-of-factly as her laughter would allow. "Maybe a nice quiet place to rest," she continued sotto voce, "but not the slammer."

Oh sure, I thought, easy for you to laugh. Easy for you to sit there—with your pants perfectly dry, with your upper thighs *not* threatening to explode, with both your shoes on, with pregnancy and childbirth a faint memory—and enjoy the humor in all this.

But as always, I rallied. Like millions of fathers before me, I found an upside in my herculean trial. As I set a course for home and drove into the falling dark, I remembered Conrad's wisdom about the sea, that it gave you a chance to feel your strength. And even though I was more tired than a human being had ever been, the sound of the children burbling away in the back seat—reliving our desperate race against the giant clock—was balm for my beleaguered soul. As they turned the day into instant legend—to be recollected I was sure as The Day Daddy Drove with No Pants—I felt my heart and lungs and quadriceps on the mend, preparing themselves for tomorrow.

Daddy Talks to God

OR

Give Me Your Tired, Your Poor, Your Hopelessly Clumsy

F amily traditions are often a Daddy ambition. From the moment my kids were born, I've hoped to pass on O'Neill family stories and customs, to keep the legend alive, maybe even buff it up a bit. Things haven't worked out exactly as I planned. I haven't always done my people proud. I have, however, learned some lessons about Christianity, Judaism, and other things to believe in.

FROM THE START, the naysayers bet against the ethnic mix of the O'Neill-Friedman parlay. The day before the wedding, the rabbi even counseled us that a Jewish-Christian marriage was "contraindicated." But we plunged ahead. We'd cobble together a melting-pot legend for the next generation.

For a time, everything went as we hoped. When the kids arrived, we lit candles at Hanukkah and told tales of Jesus. We nourished the legends of Mom's people and mine. Everything went fine, until that evening.

"Dad, am I half Jewish and half Irish?" Josh asked nervously, as though afraid it were true. Something told me this had been offered as a schoolyard slander.

Technically, the answer was yes. But I resisted the simple answer. Not just because Josh thought this was bad news, but because it seemed a dreary conclusion. After all, he wasn't Sephardic from the waist down, Celtic from there north. He wasn't some mongrel. He was, like his sister, a wholesome hybrid, blessed with the vigor of crossbreeding.

"You're not a two-flavored Popsicle, son. You're 100 percent Jewish-Irish," I said.

He looked confused and left. He came back two minutes later, carrying a Styrofoam ball. "I need a wine bottle," he chirped, sitting down between Jew and gentile. "We're supposed to make an ethnic heritage doll out of this ball and a wine bottle."

With that Jody and I took turns giving him quickie family histories. I started with the clan of Naill and threw in the colorful story of Red Hugh O'Neill, the sixteenth-century Irish lion who, at the head of a small rebel band, sent Elizabeth's Essex whimpering back to England. I closed with the history of my mother's people, the Harans, and their emigration from County Sligo before World War I. Jody then sketched the story of both the Friedmans and her maternal Stalbergs, who came from Russia around the turn of the century.

When Josh jumped up and raced excitedly back into his room, Jody and I beamed at each other, enjoying the sweet caprice that brought all those people from all those places and led to him. But then, in the same instant, we knew we had a problem.

Sure, our son could proudly carry both Celtic and Russian genes, but this Styrofoam ball/wine bottle ethnic doll would have no such DNA diversity. Would it be Jewish or Irish? A Beaujolais rabbi or a Chardonnay priest? A fugitive from Cossacks or an enemy of the queen? Dance the hora or the jig? Speak of Isaac Singer or William Yeats?

When I looked at Jody—great-granddaughter of Dora and Shmuel—I saw no self-effacement in her eyes. All the years of aspiring to blend our histories seemed suddenly naive. Cultural conflicts could yet drive us apart. When Josh came bouncing back into the room, I asked the unavoidable question.

"Can you get another Styrofoam head?"

"I'll ask Miss Cooper" was all the innocent said.

Over the next four weeks, I worked on an Irish doll with the lad and Jody worked on turning an old Zinfandel bottle into a nineteenth-century Russian Jew.

31

For the sake of the children, we feigned a familial bon-homie. But my wife and I knew this was a competition for ethnic hearts and minds. The battle was joined.

From the start it was clear that I was outgunned. Jody went to the fabric store, bought some pieces of something I think I heard her call "felt," and whipped together an authentic earth-tone peasant coat. She stuffed the little coat-arms with paper and wire. She could move them from position to position, from salute to supplication.

I taped a piece of green construction paper, skirtlike, around my bottle's midriff.

"What's that, Daddy?" Josh asked. "I don't want a lady doll."

"No, no, son," I responded in a bracing brogue, "That's a kilt, laddie. There was a time the men in Ireland wore skirts."

Josh excused himself and went into the living room. I heard him tell his mother that he'd be finished with me in a minute. When he returned, he asked me if any of the O'Neill men had ever worn pants.

"Trousers you want, trousers you'll get," I said cheerfully, picking up a pen and drawing pant legs on the little kelly-green paper tube. They didn't look exactly like a pair of Donegal tweeds. They looked more like a little kelly-green paper cylinder emblazoned with an inky upside-down *V*.

That evening as I was lying in bed and Jody went in to check on the kids, I heard a sudden guffaw from the distant room. I knew instantly that I'd left my Irish guy on Josh's desk.

"Are those supposed to be pants, Hugh?" she asked cuddling up next to me, as though she were not hysterical with superiority, but genuinely curious.

Such a question deserved no reply.

I harumphed, turned over and went to sleep.

"Not everybody took home ec in high school," I said, ten minutes later, into the silent dark of what had been a connubial bedroom before it had become a battlefield.

"I know, Hugh," the Jewess reassuringly replied. "Josh understands, too."

No question, I was overmatched here. Jody called her ninety-five-year-old grandmother and got, not only firsthand information about old Russian Jews, but a name for her bottle. She called him Isaac Garber, after her maternal great-grandfather. I named mine Mickey after, "Well," I said to Josh, "after all the Irish people whose names start with *Mc.*"

Josh laughed nervously.

Jody made Isaac a black rabbinical hat, a sort of soft-focus stovepipe job that wrapped a snug hug on his Styrofoam dome. She edged it with what I swear was a tiny piece of rabbit fur. I cut out a circle of green construction paper and stuck it into Mickey's head with a straight-pin.

"It's a tam-o'-shanter," I said, adding a second pin to accessorize.

Jody gave Isaac a great manly mustache and a beard of brown yarn. His face had both a Mongol swagger and the sadness of the ages. That night, I tried to steal the yarn but couldn't find her stash. I gave Mickey a blue ballpoint beard.

Jody even made Isaac a little scarf, with fringe that apparently had religious significance, and a tiny Talmud that he cradled against his bosom. When she pointed out that my guy was in no identifiable way Irish, I solved the problem with mucilage and a small placard. "England out of Ireland," it read.

"God help you," my wife said.

Eventually, Jody produced a stunning rendition of shtetl life in the Caucasus. I, on the other hand, had fashioned a totem that would have given a therapist the willies. That realization broke my heart. It was not for this that my people had made their way to America—so their grandson could depict them in Day-Glo pants with royal blue beards. That evening in my prayers I apologized to all the Harans and O'Neills.

Fortunately for me, the school Christmas break called a temporary cease-fire to the dueling diaspora dolls.

A revelation about the Irish and the Jews was at hand.

IT WAS Saint Stephen's Night, also known as December 26, the day after Christmas. We were in the first row of the balcony of the Gershwin Theater, Broadway and Fifty-first. Below us *Fiddler on the Roof* was unfolding. The Jews of Anatevka were singing of the day the Messiah would come.

"Dad," said Josh tugging at my sleeve in the dark, "I thought yesterday was the Messiah's birthday."

"Well, it was, Josh," I began, "but the Jews believe . . ." Then I decided this might take some time.

"I'll explain it after the show," I said without a clue as to how I would demystify such matters.

But trust me, later that night I was nothing short of brilliant. I subdued my competitiveness with Jody and not only rendered but honored both the Christian faith—the world as redeemed once already—and the Jewish one—keep the faith, there is milk and honey on the other side. Indeed, I managed to present them as not in conflict at all, any more than a person's left hand is in conflict with his right. The world of spirit isn't either-or, went my subtext. It is an inquiry, a sifting. If reason can't answer ineffable questions, then faith will make us strong.

"That's interesting, Dad," Josh said, as I tucked him in and finished my interfaith peroration. "What does *effable* mean?"

"Ineffable—it means 'confounding,'" I said. "You know, 'hard to understand.'"

"I want the Jews to be right," he said, after a moment's thought.

"What do you mean?"

"I hope the Messiah hasn't come yet," he said.

My heart broke. What he meant was that he hoped things could, and would, be better, that someday children wouldn't taunt each other with ethnic salvos and that someday he and I wouldn't argue. He hoped, like Tevye, that truth and justice would appear on earth, that there were sweeter days ahead.

Looking down at him in that instant, I could imagine no more potent an engine for a life than the Christian-Jewish dynamo, the paired-but-opposite ideas that the Messiah has come and gone, that the world is sanctified already, and that the world will someday be better if we continue to trust the Lord. On behalf of my kids and my wife, I vowed to keep our particular switch-hitting covenant and thanked whatever gods there may be for an earth both full of blessings and ripe with yet-to-comes.

When the kids returned to school after the holidays, I couldn't blame Josh for giving Isaac Garber the nod when it came time to bring in his ethnic project.

As Jody was packing a carton labeled "Heritage Box" for Josh to take to school, I noticed—squeezed in with Isaac, among the homemade blintzes, the caviar, the facsimile Russian religious artifacts—Jody had included a tape of the Clancy Brothers' greatest hits.

"What's this, Mommy?" Josh said, holding up the tape.

"That's the sound of Daddy's people," she replied. "Play it for the kids. They'll love it."

Three days later, when I came upon Josh zapping bad guys in some video game, he was humming the Irish anthem "Roddy McCauley." The ruddy summons of the pipes had taken root.

I may have let my people down, but their great-granddaughter-in-law, whose people were from the Ukraine, had not.

Daddy Gets Hungry

OR

That's No Weasel, That's My Dad

Whenever possible, I like to believe anything good about fatherhood. For example, I want to believe the scientific studies which show that fathers tend to live a tad longer than men without kids. But they can't be right. They're clearly just a case of sentiment driving science. Researchers *want* to believe that the emotional consolations of family life have a life-extending effect. So their studies suggest just that.

Fact: Any possible health benefit of family life, of prolonged exposure to kid laughter, is far outweighed by the nutritional downside of being around kid food. I ask you, If you're selling term-life for Allstate, who's your preferred risk,

> (A) the childless guy who just had a radicchio salad and a nice piece of fish with his wife,

or

(B) the daddy who just snacked on a Ring Ding
he found behind the video games?

Fact: Petrified snack food is bad news for life
expectancy.

Before I had kids, I was, I admit, no poster boy for
the American Heart Association. On occasion, I ate
steak rare and enjoyed a spud with sour cream. But
now the only thing rare in my life is a normal meal.
Sorry to report, I've traded the mature pleasures of
cholesterol and carnivorousness for spun sugar and
food coloring.

Bad deal.

The juveniling of my diet started early—three
months into fatherhood—when I reached into the
fridge to quench a midnight thirst and bolted down
baby formula Jody had poured into a milk glass. Try
to imagine drinking a sweater.

Things went downhill food-wise from there. For a
few weeks when Josh was six, I was addicted to a
sandwich he called a "fluffernutter"—peanut butter
and marshmallow fluff. Eventually, I actually ate
something called a Pudding-Rollup, a little blanket of
pudding, woven—I can only assume—from pudding
fibers. I devolved, in short, from a somewhat sophisti-

cated grown man into a guy who made a big deal out of spelling "knuckle" with alphabet soup.

But serious as it is, the story of how fatherhood changes *what* you eat is trivial compared to its effect on *how* you eat. The Daddy-changes in eating style can lead to a gradual erosion of your self-esteem that undermines not just your health, but your marriage and your career.

Every internist in the world will tell you that the dinner hour should be a calm interlude. I wish I could tell you that at dinnertime we pass the cauliflower and beans and gab, drawing sustenance from each of the food groups and each other. But I can't tell you that.

Here's what I can tell you. Any food *one* of my kids likes provokes a gag reflex in the other. Rebecca likes noodles mushy and Josh is an al dente kind of guy. Josh loves cheddar cheese; the girl-child thinks it's poison. Further, Rebecca is phobic about different foods touching each other. If a carrot stick should brush a drumstick, she wants to dial 911. Consequently, dinner is not always Norman Rockwellian.

The fact is that seven nights out of ten, I "dine" standing at the sink while rinsing the sixty-eight plates on which I've offered the kids every conceivable food in search of something, anything they'd eat that was vaguely nutritious for them. I spritz the dishes and scavenge the remains. The scene ain't for the faint of heart.

No use letting those six noodles go to waste.

And hey, that's perfectly good applesauce the kids sneered at.

Oops, Becky left a chicken stick.

One night, I had a dinner of eight Spaghetti-os, a dollop of yogurt, half an Oreo, a raisin, a thumbful of ketchup, and a Wilma Flintstone vitamin pellet.

I like to think I eat what the kids pass up because I'm an ecologist, determined not to waste the world's abundance. But that's not it at all. Rather, I've lost all semblance of self-control. Undone by disappointment—the fact that even the lollapalooza lasagna I so lovingly prepared was a flop—I've simply gone rogue. I am no frugal maximizer of Mother Earth. No, I'm a kitchen weasel, slurping up detritus: shreds of chicken, a tomato skin, a single Frosted Flake, leftover nibbles and bites. My version of a balanced meal is one that comes from at least six plates.

I reached the depths one summer night. Alone amid the postmeal wreckage, I gathered and rinsed and wiped—plates, counters, mayonnaise off my wrist. Then, damp sponge in hand, I bent down to clean under the table.

I remember whisking at a few crumbs under Josh's chair. I remember a pea hiding by the table leg. And I remember a noodle, a corkscrew twist. I swept, no clawed, it up with my fingers. And then, with no place to put it, I—God help me—popped the perky piece of pasta into my mouth and swallowed. As all hope disappeared, I remember thinking that carpet fiber was probably not the kind most doctors recommend.

Daddy Defends His Turf

OR

Of Private Property and Fighting Plaque

> All changed, changed utterly,
> A terrible beauty is born.
> —*William Butler Yeats*

Most literary scholars believe that those famous Yeats lines refer to the political revolution in Ireland in 1916. They're wrong. They actually refer to a far more dramatic change in Yeats's life—becoming a father. Indeed, in an early draft of the poem, the now famous couplet read a little differently: "All changed, changed utterly / A terrible *cutey* is born."

Becoming a father changes everything. And I do mean everything: the way you speak, the way you work, sleep, drive, eat, dress, think. It even changes what you sing. Fatherhood changes your posture, your sex life, your hairstyle, your feelings about money, politics, God, about your past, and about the planet's future. Children change the ground you walk on. Elizabeth Stone said it best. "The decision to have a child," she wrote, "is momentous. It is to decide forever to have your heart go walking around outside your body."

My kids have certainly changed me. They have made me into one very possessive man.

I used to be no more nor less concerned about my "things" than the next guy. But now I am positively nuts about protecting my "stuff," psychotic about guarding my goods. Why have I become such a lunatic? Simple. Because the kids have launched a full-frontal attack on every object I ever called my own.

Submitted for your consideration:

Item 1: On my fortieth birthday, my brother gave me a pen I cherish for both its source and its heft. It's a manly implement, a tool with which a fella might write an honest sentence or two. And though I keep it carefully in its case in my top desk drawer, I have found it, over the last three years, just about everywhere else: on the chalk ledge in a first-grade classroom, taped to a poster as the centerpiece of a school project called "The History of Writing," and with Colonel Mustard and the candlestick inside the Clue box.

Why do the kids take my pen? And not any of the skillion sixty-nine-cent ballpoints or number-two pencils on my desk? Only God can know.

Item 2: I have one incredibly expensive silk tie on which I had spent an entire week's salary back when I was a lad in Manhattan. I had done it in an attempt to prove—to myself—that I was confident about my prospects in The City That Never Sleeps. It's the most beautiful necktie in the history of the world.

Rebecca is incapable of keeping her mitts off it.

When she walked on-stage in the role of the Indian maid Sacajawea, her headband looked familiar. She once used my tie to hobble her cousins for the three-legged race. She even used it as a leash the weekend we babysat for the neighbor's dog.

Why? you ask. Why? Why does Rebecca always borrow the one tie about which I care a fig? Why doesn't she, just once, reach into my closet and pull out my pea-soup-green polyester number with the bucking broncos on it?

Ask God.

Item 3: Eight out of ten mornings, when I reach for my toothbrush, it's gone. Vanished. Gone. Eight out of ten mornings, I can't even fight the war against gum disease without first searching the house.

I have found my toothbrush virtually everywhere. In the basement on top of the humidifier. Being used as a bookmark in a copy of *James and the Giant Peach*. I once found it on Josh's desk next to a coin-collecting folder and a numismatic pamphlet about getting tarnish off nickels.

Why? you may ask. What possible reason could the kids have for taking my toothbrush from its little ceramic holster where it hung so handily over the sink? Ask the devil; maybe he'll understand. All I know is that it's enough to make a man a little fussy about his things.

I've tried every conceivable tone of voice to keep the kids away from my pen, my tie, and my toothbrush. I've threatened. I've begged. Nothing works. Josh traded my pen to his friend Kyle for a Ken Griffey Jr. rookie card.

Eventually, I came to believe that the kids weren't really to blame. Call me a softy, but I actually believe that they're not in control of their actions. I believe they're in thrall to some ancient, seditious kid instinct to test Daddy, to gnaw away at even the small pleasures that sustain the old man, to push him to the limit to see what he's made of.

They're trying to teach me, you see. They're trying to teach me that "things" are unimportant, that possessions are corrupt, that wanting your own toothbrush is decadent and self-indulgent.

And you know what? I have actually achieved some self-knowledge from their assault on my stuff. In fact, the morning I found my toothbrush in the hamster cage, I learned something very important about myself: I hate the taste of wood chips in the morning.

Daddy Gets a Trim

OR

The Covenant of the Crewcut

EB. White once said that as a writer he felt charged with the safekeeping of all unexpected enchantments, as though he might be held personally responsible if even a small one were to be lost. When you're chasing children around, your life gets positively lousy with small "enchantments."

Once you have kids, every plain thing is burnished by youth. To a father, nothing is only what it appears. The search for a left mitten is a philosophical occasion. Even a boy's summertime haircut is an annual communion.

JOSH CALLS HIS summer haircut by its modern name, the spike. But, believe me, there is nothing the slightest bit hip about the style. It's a good old-fashioned crewcut, a buzz, a close-cropped honey that would have made a drill instructor from Fort Drum get misty.

His crewcut always feels to me less like a head of hair than like a pelt. Every June, as we leave the barbershop and I rub my hand over the sharp bristle, I get a powerful sense of the boy as a creature, a young otter growing into his eventual shape.

The most interesting thing about Josh's crewcut is that people can't help touching it. Strangers on the street reach out and rub his head as though for luck. The buzz cut is a summertime talisman. Suddenly, head all shorn, that American face just jumps out at you. Every expression—of either exuberance or woe— is immediate, crystal clear. There are no shadows, no places for anything to hide. That plain old boy's head, those ears, those freckles, that brand-new, right-out-there face is a reminder of sweet things, like brothers and neighbor kids.

This is no mere haircut, I tell you. It is a prayer that kids can be plain and happy and young and easy. It is not just a haircut. It is a tribute to summer in this favored land.

Daddy Gets Slandered

OR

Of Millionaires, Misers, and Me

Fathers take a lot of bad raps. The stereotype that bugs me most is the cheapskate slander, the cliché of Dad as the penny-pinching old man. This libel runs deep in the American grain, shows itself in countless sitcoms, even in the greatest play in the history of American theater. Eugene O'Neill's *Long Day's Journey into Night* revolves around a parsimonious papa who not only turns off lights compulsively but skimps on Mom's hospitalization.

My kids buy into this ignoble American slander. Behind my back, they accuse me of being "frugal." Only they don't use euphemisms. They use the C word. Dad's cheap. C-h-e-a-p. That's what they whisper in the dark.

One night, after I had refused to give them a quarter to use a bowling ball polisher to shine a bowling ball that actually belonged to White Plains Lanes, I over-heard Rebecca compare me to Scrooge McDuck, Donald Duck's skinflint uncle. Her brother polished the joke: "Scrooge McDad," Josh christened me.

This wasn't exactly the image I was going for. And for a time, I was upset that my kids saw me that way. But eventually, once I tracked down the source of the Shylock smear, I realized that it actually revealed me as a *good* father.

It all started, you see, with the O'Neill Air Conditioner Rule.

THE O'NEILL Air Conditioner Rule goes as follows: Any family member may turn an air conditioner off; only a parent can turn an air conditioner on.

Now the kids think this rule exists because I'm obsessed with high utility bills. Not so. Money has nothing to do with the rule, which grew out of something much bigger than money—specifically my hope that my kids will one day be functional members of society. To explain, I've got to start with our differing attitudes toward air conditioners, first mine, then the kids'.

I confess to thinking that in the suburbs of New York air conditioners are a decadent, energy-wasting, ozone-layer-destroying indulgence. (Please note that the word "expensive" does not appear.) Nonetheless, even *I* will grant that there are a handful of days in midsummer when it makes sense to crank up the a/c.

Josh and Rebecca have a slightly different attitude, best summarized thusly: "Oh, Dad, please, turn it on! Now, Dad, please! I'll die. P-l-e-a-s-e, I'm dying. It's so hot." Usually, right after Christmas, they start lobbying for a few BTUs.

Once on New Year's Eve, Rebecca told me her stuffed animals were hot. "You know, Dad, polar bears can die from warmness," she said holding up Moby Bear in a shameless attempt to exploit his cuteness. Josh once offered me a pro-air-conditioning petition that began "When in the course of *humid* events." All he got was admiration of the word play.

"Nice pun, son," I said.

Now lest you judge me harshly, let me remind you that we are not a State Department family stationed outside Rio. We are not in Panama City, Florida. No, we live in the northern temperate zone, about a three-iron south of the Saint Lawrence Seaway. And yet my kids are always on the brink of heat stroke.

Last February I was watching the eleven o'clock news when Josh arrived in the den, fanning himself and virtually naked. He was covered in what I was supposed to believe was sweat.

"Dad, please, I beg you. Turn on the a/c!"

I asked him if he had by any chance splashed himself with water to simulate malaria-induced perspiration.

"Believe me, Dad," he said, "I'm too hot to even *think* of it."

"Go to bed, son," I said, "And if you start to feel feverish, just lick your arms and legs."

"Daaaaad," he said, as though he suspected I wasn't taking his predicament seriously.

"No, really," I went on, the master of Dad sarcasm. "It's an old Laotian survival technique."

"Daaaad," he whined again.

"No kidding," I said. "It drops the body temp. People in the Yukon use it to survive those sweltering Arctic Circle summers."

After he turned and left, I heard a thump from the hallway that sounded like a boy collapsing in a dehydrated heap. I aimed my remote control and clicked to the Knicks-Rockets game.

Sometimes the kids even enlisted their friends in their cause. One night the phone rang.

"Hello, Mr. O'Neill," said seven-year-old Kate from next door, "Becky said to tell you that my daddy lets me put on the air conditioner whenever I want."

"Thanks for your input, doll," I said. Now there's a waste of a message unit, I thought.

Anyway, here's how the a/c controversy proves that I'm a good father.

The easiest thing for me to do would be to fold my hands and give the kids carte blanche on the a/c. For an extra hundred bucks a year, which I have, I could stop worrying that Josh's memoir of his youth will be called *Notes of a Miser's Boy*. But I won't take the easy way. And I repeat: My hard line on air conditioning has absolutely nothing to do with money. Nor does it have to do with environmental awareness. Even if I had a gazillion dollars and fluorocarbons were good for the atmosphere, I'd still play gatekeeper on the a/c switch.

Why?

Because air conditioning is just too easy. It's a quick fix.

Little humid? Bang—hit the button.

Life has an obstacle or two? Hey, where's the button?

I won't make the argument that hardship builds character, only that air conditioning does not.

Trust me. I am no drill instructor. I've never made the kids run overland with a full pack. Or drop and give me forty. The only toughness I have ever demanded is enough grit to endure a July night in Mercer County, New Jersey, without begging for an IV drip?

Look at it this way: If a father didn't see to it that his kids learned to read, he'd be irresponsible, right? Well, what about the father who sends his kids out into the world incapable of going to sleep anywhere south of the tundra without a GE humming in the window? Has that father failed his child? You bet he has.

Besides, if all these predictions about global warming come true, only folks who are good in the heat will prosper. And hey, if I can get the kids ready for the future and save a few bucks in the process, no use making the electric company any richer.

Daddy Gets a Reality Check

OR

A Mary Poppins Meditation

Anybody who has ever tried to lead any enterprise knows the value of a good slogan. The brains at Yale draw strength from Lux et Veritas (Light and Truth). Tug McGraw's "Ya gotta believe" sustained the New York Mets through the pennant race of 1973. Perhaps the most useful Daddy phrase of all time comes from the Disney film version of *Mary Poppins*.

GEORGE BANKS, aka Father, is the British Empire in a derby; he sings songs about compound interest. While Mary Poppins, the kids' somewhat unconventional nanny, shares his enthusiasm for efficiency, she also thinks life has room for buoyance and business.

One day she bamboozles Dad into taking the kids to work with him, mixing family with finance. There is, of course, an immediate run on the Fidelity Fiduciary

Bank. And Dad gets in deep Dutch with the boss, the dour Mister Dawes. Asked to explain himself to a bank tribunal, a court-martial of commerce, George Banks surprises himself and uses Mary's preposterous word *supercalifragilisticexpialidocious*.

"There's no such word!" Dawes snaps.

"With all due respect, sir," the suddenly liberated Dad replies, "there's no such thing as you," and everybody is next seen flying a kite in the park.

George hit it on the screws. The covenant with our kids is so bright that it moves the rest of the world into the shadows. When you find yourself face-to-face with your children, called on to comfort them, to teach them, to scold them, to exhort them, to allay their fears, you feel a freshness in your soul. Business falls away. Opinion falls away. Everything you think you know about the world out there seems derived, secondhand compared to your knowledge of your kids. Facing a child, you feel as though this is happening to you and only you. That experience is authentic. The others seem once removed.

I often think that the only thing I know for sure, for dead-solid, no-doubt-about-it sure, is what I know about my children. Though that knowledge is ineffable and beyond description, it is nonetheless certain and bone deep. These kids are indeed supercalifragilisticexpialidocious, Mr. Dawes. There is no such thing as you.

Daddy Is a Teacher

OR

Of Two-Wheelers and One Lesson

Buried not-so-deep in the subconscious of most fathers is an idealized image of Dad the Teacher, the man who passes on knowledge. It's a remnant of a time when parents actually taught children survival skills, how to hunt and fish, plant and harvest, build a life with their hands. I have paternal fantasies of teaching Josh and Rebecca all kinds of skills—how to use a band saw, how to groom an Airedale, how to sail into the wind.

Unfortunately, I don't know how to do any of those things myself. In fact, I don't know how to do much of anything. I know nothing about surviving in the woods. Less than nothing about first aid. I don't know how to whittle, tie knots, fight crabgrass, or plumb-bob anything. I'm not exactly a storehouse of know-how. About the only things I know how to do are make chili and jump-start a car.

For a while, it troubled me. I worried that an incompetent Dad could only raise incompetent kids. But then one afternoon, flat on my back on the pavement in a Manhattan playground, I realized it ain't necessarily so. I realized I knew everything I had to know to teach my kids the most important lesson there is.

JOSH WAS JUST six years old. We were at the park, late on one of those golden, New York October afternoons. Strangers were playing basketball together. Tape players dueled—salsa and Debussy—as old men played chess in the falling light. And in one corner of this sweet city tumult, Josh and I were going one-on-one with a two-wheeler. The training wheels had been taken off. A rite of passage was in the air.

I was playing the time-honored Daddy role—running beside Josh, one hand on the back of the saddle, the other on a handlebar—steadying him as he gained speed, then launching him.

"Try to keep your weight balanced," I said.

He was playing the traditional kid role—human cannonball. With each attempted takeoff, the problem was the same. No sooner would I let go of him than Josh would panic, stop pedaling—thereby losing vital forward momentum—wobble left, overcorrect to the right, and crash to the blacktop with a yelp.

I told him to keep pedaling through the wobble and turn the handlebars more gently. But no luck. Each time his flight path was the same. Over and over. He couldn't seem to turn the advice into action. He was, however, dogged. He always got up and tried again. Despite the banged knees and scraped elbows, the boy kept getting back on this horse. Then, after about a half-hour of tumbles to the pavement, the break-through moment arrived.

Once again, I ran alongside and let him go. Once again, he wobbled left and in a panic overcorrected right. But then, the good news. He corrected back to the left again and then once more—this time, gently— back to the right. What's more, he pedaled throughout and found his equilibrium.

Ten yards, twenty yards, thirty yards. Behind him, I was hunkered down on the pavement, exhausted from all that running, bent over at the waist. Josh made a sound that one word cannot properly describe. It was a gasp-whimper-laugh-shout-cry for help, at once euphoric and terrified, a beautiful, eureka sound. His little shoulders were hunched up in elation and dread. Josh was going, on his own, out there on the high wire.

Finally after a journey of fifty yards, he ran out of room, rode softly into the chain-link fence, and fell over. He jumped up and left his bike, wheel spinning by the fence, and raced toward me, more excited than a *Homo sapiens* had ever been.

"Daddy, did you see?" he shouted. "Did you see?"

"Yeah, that was great, man, great!" I cried as he ran toward me, aglow with what he had done. When he reached me, he was far too excited to slow down. Instead, he charged right into me at full six-year-old speed and knocked me over backward like one of those roly-poly dolls.

"Daddy, I rode all the way over there!" he said, lying on top of me, pointing to the fence.

"I know," I said. "You were flying!"

"Did you see, Dad? Did you see!" He was on fire. He was breathless. He was laughing. He was thumping my chest with his fists. He was lit from within.

Something in him understood that this was his first *achievement*, the first thing to which he had given energy and time. This was the first thing he could be said to have *accomplished*. And lying there underneath him, looking into his shining face, I suddenly realized that even a father who didn't know much could teach his kids an important truth.

True enough, I couldn't show my kids how to rebuild a carburetor, put up dry wall, fly fish, till a field, or take up a hem. But I could point them to possibilities. I could make them believe in effort and attention. I could make them dauntless.

I could make a big deal out of human achievement, not just in biking or sports or politics, but in parenting and woodcarving, friendship, flute-playing, marketing, opera, juggling, speaking with style, cooking, gardening, even writing. I could make it my job to celebrate the catalog of things people can learn to do. I could, at every opportunity, make it clear that though the world is often cantankerous, it is just as often susceptible to brains and energy and will. I might not be able to do much myself, but I could commend my kids to the glory of human beings at full throttle. I could teach them to keep pedaling.

Daddy Meets Einstein

OR

The Physics of Fatherhood

Becoming a father helped me solve one of the great mysteries of science. I've got the explanation of black holes in deep space, those regions where gravity is so strong that not even light can escape. There can be only one possible explanation.

Somehow vast groups of children have been lashed together and suspended in the far reaches of the universe.

How do I know? Simple. Only children generate so powerful a gravitational field. Only children can suck you so completely into their misadventures. Only children can swallow a man whole. You want evidence? I'll give you evidence. Try all the times I've been sucked into doing fourth-grade book reports, sucked into night terrors, sucked into arguments over a blue crayon, sucked into a search for a puppet's hat. Try all

those science fairs that have taught me another startling fact, this one about parenthood's link to quantum physics.

"DEAR MOMS AND Dads," the paper Josh carried
home from school began. "The first-grade science fair
will be held on April 5." It was a typically joyful docu-
ment, encouraging parental involvement and suggest-
ing a few age-appropriate projects. After a little
brainstorming, Josh and I decided we would trace the
history of a daisy, from seed to full flower. "The Biog-
raphy of a Plant," we dubbed our project.

Over the next two weeks we spent fifteen minutes
every day working together on a kid-friendly rendition of Mother Nature's cycle of fertility, nurturance,
and growth. The centerpiece of the project was a
poster on which we illustrated each of the daisy stages:

> Upper left (panel one): a dirt-filled flowerpot
> drawn by Josh
>
> Upper right (panel two): the same pot with some
> fingers entering from off-camera sprinkling daisy
> seeds
>
> Middle left (panel three): rain drops (I suggested
> that the rain should fall at an angle. "Looks like a
> storm," Josh said happily.)

Middle right (panel four): rays of sun warming everything to life (Josh discovered that rays of sunshine looked hotter if you made the lines wavy.)

Panels five and six: sprout and flower

Finally, we collaborated on a poem to encapsulate the water-warmth-blossom cycle of botanical life:

> Some seeds and some sunshine,
> Some drops from the sky,
> And up comes a daisy—
> Sweet to the eye.

In the interests of hands-on learning, we prepared two three-dimensional models: of panel one, an actual plastic flowerpot with potting soil, and of panel five, an identical dirt-filled pot with a little green frond, made of construction paper, peeking effusively up from the earth. By the time April 5 rolled around, we were ready.

The gym was a bright chaos. As parents and kids set up their science projects, the teachers cruised among the tables spreading scientific cheer. To our left, a father and son were unboxing a multicomponent computer system of some sort. The father opened a little felt pouch, revealing a set of small tools, and he set to work assembling. The son turned to us.

"Hi, Josh," he said.

"Hi, Jeremy," Josh replied. "What's your project?"

"A computerized model of Mount Saint Helens."

"The volcano?" Josh asked, looking back over his shoulder at me for reassurance that our poster was great. I smiled weakly.

"Does it explode?" Josh went on.

"Yeah," said Jeremy, as his father slithered under the table to connect something to something else. "What's yours?"

"The Life Cycle of a Daisy," Josh answered, walking over to Jeremy's Dad, who was, I think, linking the computer via a pneumatic tube to a perfect model mountain range.

"What's that?" Josh asked, pointing to a small speck on the side of a slope.

"A bighorn sheep," said Jeremy.

"Species name?" Jeremy's Dad quizzed him from under the table.

"*Ovis canedensis*," said the boy.

As Josh walked, intrigued, around to the front of the tabletop volcano, he accidentally knocked over our three-D of panel five. Some potting soil splashed out of the flowerpot, and our construction paper "sprout" fluttered to the gym floor. Jeremy picked up the little green shred.

"You need this?" he asked, as though it were just some little green shred and not the beginning of life itself. As I repotted our bud, Jeremy continued his explanation of the mini-Mount Saint Helens.

"You use the keyboard to increase the geothermal pressure. You hit the up-arrow over and over again."

On the computer screen, there was a cross section of the mountain with an ominous, bulging pressure-bubble near its base.

As Jeremy tapped the cursor arrow, the bubble got bigger and bigger. Apparently, pressure was building.

"Okay, Dad?" Jeremy asked, looking for the go-ahead.

"Just one sec, kiddo," said Mr. Daddy Genius, packing something into the back of the mountain range. "Okay, pal, let 'er rip."

Jeremy hit the up-arrow. There was a computer sound-effect rumble, and on the screen the underground bubble strained and burst.

Then over in the bonsai Cascade range, the peak of one of the mountains blew off, shooting upward toward the gym ceiling, a geological jump ball. A geyser of ash erupted from the mountain, and after a second, a stream of glowing orange lava surged out of the peak and down the slope.

Instantly, children and parents gathered from all over the gym. As a river of lava slithered down the hillside knocking over the little minitrees in its path, rubberneckers crowded around, fascinated by disaster.

"Awesome," said a girl in pink jeans.

A red-headed boy reached out to touch the lava.

"Careful," said Jeremy. "It's hot."

I laughed, looking over at Jeremy's Dad in fellowship. Not enough to build them a computerized volcano, my expression said, they have to pretend the lava is hot.

"Ow," yelped Rusty, shaking his fingers and disappearing into the crowd.

The lava oozed off the table and onto my wingtips. To this day, I haven't gotten all of the neon orange goop out of the tiny decorative holes.

Later that day, as everybody was packing up the projects, the principal came up to me and said with clear interest in Josh. "Mr. O'Neill, you know, you should feel free to help Josh with his science projects. He may need a little more guidance than some of the other children."

I had no idea how to respond. Only one thing was clear. I was not about to admit that I was the "brains" behind the daisy display.

"He's the sweetest boy," she went on, "and it was an adorable project. But some kids need a helping hand."

"Oh sure," I said. "Next year, I'll help him. This month was just crazy for me."

IN THE YEARS that followed, I became obsessed with the school science fair. I went beyond giving Josh a "little more guidance." In fact, I started taking my vacation the two weeks prior to the big event, just so I could spend some time in the basement tinkering. Jeremy's father had a Ph.D. in fluid dynamics from CalTech. I clearly couldn't out-think him, so I decided to outwork him.

Each year, I made some progress. In second grade, I came up with a centrifugal-force project. The teaching device was a pair of pantyhose with a microscopic hole cut in one foot. By dropping an ordinary household golf ball down the leg, then whirling the nylons overhead, centrifugal force would tear open the hole and send the Titleist 2 screaming across the gym.

From the beginning Josh was skeptical. He called Jeremy.

"Oh, we're using my mom's underwear," Josh said flatly into the phone, "to show *sensual* force."

"No, no, no," I corrected him, grabbing the phone. "That's *centrifugal* force, *centrifugal*."

Let's just say, things did not work out as I had planned. After a golf ball—flying off on a tangent—hit the school dietitian in the shin, Josh and I were asked to stop whipping the hosiery around and take our exhibit outside. Nobody noticed when we left. They were all lined up to try Jeremy's zero-gravity chamber.

In third grade, we offered "The Festival of Leverage," a project built around a paint-stick-and-spool fulcrum.

That year, Jeremy did an in vitro fertilization.

In fourth grade, the O'Neills presented "This Accident Called Science" featuring an apple just like the one that fell on Isaac Newton's head and a cup of cottage cheese demonstrating the food spoilage that led to penicillin.

Jeremy found the universe's missing mass.

And brought it to school.

In fifth grade, I did my best work. Created an eighteen-foot-wide model of the solar system, complete with retrograde rotation and Martian canals.

Jeremy cloned his cousin.

WHEN I WAS doing some background research for the sixth grade fair, I read about a scientific principle that was almost a consolation prize for all my humiliations: the Heisenberg Uncertainty Principle. The dictionary defines the principle of quantum mechanics thusly: "the accurate measurement of one of two related quantities, as position and momentum or energy and time produce uncertainties in the measurement of the other." In other words, you can either determine exactly where a quark is or you can measure how fast it's moving. You can't do both. At least, not precisely. Try to and guess what? You'll ending up having to deal with "uncertainties in both quantities equal to or greater than h/2, where h equals Planck's constant."

This guy Heisenberg must have had kids. His principle is a pretty good description of parenthood. Parenthood *is* uncertainty. I always figure out what my kids need from me just as they no longer need it. If I can determine their position precisely, I miss how fast they're going. All the million moments of affection and impatience get mushed together.

Science and parenthood are hard.

Daddy Breaks a Record

OR

Of Ligaments and Light Speed

Mothers don't do waterslides. Or not much anyway. Check out the line at any of the venues on the eastern seaboard waterpark circuit—from Aquaboggan in Saco, Maine, to Typhoon Lagoon in Orlando—and you'll see 90 percent kids and 10 percent *fathers*. Very few mothers. Mom is usually holding the shirts and shoes.

But Dads are drawn to waterslides. Indeed there is a quiet fraternity among fluming fathers. As we waddle past each other—dripping wet, carrying our foam pads—we often nod in acknowledgment, knights on a shared quest. But for what? What is the Holy Grail we're after?

That's what I was thinking as I lowered myself keister-first into launch-mode at the top of the slide. Positioning my raft in the foam, I peered down the flume, tucked my knees up by my chin, checked my launch angle, and wondered, once again, what strange compulsion had led me to become—at midlife—a waterslide cowboy?

None of the conventional thrill-seeking explanations rang true. The mountain climber's "Because it's there" seemed shallow. I stretched forward and grabbed the sides of the slide and pulled powerfully, propelling myself into the plunge. As I sluiced down the turquoise tube, I was no longer a person, no longer Hugh O'Neill, but just another anonymous 175-pound Newtonian mass helpless in gravity's thrall. As I banked into the first turn, the question mocked me.

Why? What exactly was I chasing?

Halfway through the second turn, I was high on the side wall and moving at Mach 1 when it happened. My raft somehow turned sideways and I lost speed. Not much, but just enough, I instantly knew, to keep me from holding my nice high line through the curve. I fell off the wall and thwumped/crashed—left shoulder first—into the bottom of the slide. I doubted I'd be able to reach an orthopedist on the weekend.

As I came around the final turn into the straightaway to splashdown, I caught sight of Josh and Rebecca waiting for me in the pool at the bottom of the slide. In a freeze-frame, I saw them both with sublime clarity: Rebecca, pushing her hair back from her face, a green-eyed sprite, shiny and slick as a seal pup; Josh, hefting his own rubber raft before him, looking back up the slide for Dad. I could feel his goodness, his youth, and an incredible throbbing in my shoulder.

But I suddenly knew the answer to the question. I knew what I was after. I knew what I was chasing.

I was after my children.

So much of what they feel is inaccessible to me. I am hopelessly removed from the alertness of being a child. And they have no clue about the burdens of being me. So often when they talk, I'm groping for what they mean. Language fails them; sympathy fails me. But this slide was a shared language. This slide was common ground. When they talk about the dread of Meet-Your-Maker Falls I know precisely what they mean. I've been there. I've felt the G forces and the spray.

At the moment of splashdown, I whooped and cried out in real pain, which the kids thought was a phony fear. They laughed. And we were together, inhabiting precisely the same moment of goofy exultation. It was perfectly clear what I had been chasing.

Daddy Gets Tackled

OR

Of an Old Lion and Baby Cubs

Rebecca christened the game "fallball." Not because we first played it in the autumn, but because its point was simply to *fall* on the *ball* and hold on as long as you could. The game wasn't really invented; it just arrived in our lives.

We were playing football at Jody's parents' house outside Philadelphia when Josh fumbled at midfield. Rebecca and I both went for the loose ball. Since her reflexes were six years old and mine were close to forty, she covered the ball in a nanosecond, just as my brain was telling my body to bend over. In mock annoyance, I grabbed at the ball underneath her and did some play-by-play.

"Rebecca's on top of the ball, but it looks like Daddy is going to take it away from her. Yes, folks, Daddy's got a grip on the ball and is going to tear it from his daughter's grasp and score a touchdown."

"My ball, Daddy!" Rebecca yelped.

"Hey," Josh shouted. "You can't do that. Our ball."

"No," I shouted, still an announcer. "The rules of football have suddenly been changed and now it's legal to steal the ball when a kid is lying on top of it."

With that I took the ball, jumped up, and headed for pay dirt. The kids were outraged and amused.

"Hey, come back here," Rebecca howled from the turf. "You can't do that."

"Yes, I can," I shouted over my shoulder as I jogged toward the goal line near the garage. And then in a flash of inspiration, I made a great Daddy move. I deliberately fumbled the ball. And more important, I continued my best play-by-play.

"But Daddy fumbles and the ball is loose in the middle of the field."

The instant Josh and Rebecca and I all darted toward the ball, fallball was born. We arrived at the same moment. I once again bent over awkwardly. But the kids both made big-time athletic moves. Rebecca dove headlong, fully extended like a flying squirrel, toward the ball. Josh did a feet-first slide, screening me away from the ball with his body in a move that would have done a free safety for the 49ers proud.

But the ball skittered away from them and I managed to drop my 175-pound bulk on the ball. And I do mean *drop.* I wasn't interested in advancing the ball. I took a possession position. I was a dead-weight, paternal hulk, curled up on top of the pigskin.

A second later, the kids landed on top of me and the central struggle of fallball revealed itself. Josh and Rebecca set to work trying to pry the ball loose. For the next five minutes, they just plain pummeled me, working me over like a pair of welterweights. They rained blows on me, thumping my back with their puny fists. They tried to burrow, squirm under me, and grab the ball. Since I was so big, they clearly thought this should be no-holds-barred. So they tickled me and twisted my ears. Torn between ferocity and laughter, they also showed some nice teamwork.

"Becky," Josh said through gritted teeth, "you pull his arm. I'll bend back his fingers."

Then I made another astute Daddy move. I let them think they had overpowered me, contriving to have the ball squirt suddenly free, out from under the pile of us.

The kids screamed and it was off to the races after the ball. Rebecca got there first and curled up on top of the ball like a corduroy hedgehog. She was squeezing the life out of the football and giggling uncontrollably.

I loomed over her and threatened in my best ogre voice. "Give me that ball!" I roared.

"No way," she said, defiant and helpless with glee.

"I want my ball," I roared again, falling down on all fours over her. She screamed and wrapped her legs around the ball as well.

From that day forward, for about two years, whenever any one of us would merely toss the football onto the lawn, within minutes we'd all be grappling for possession in a pile, together in a free-for-all family scrimmage.

The fallball highlight film is etched in memory. I remember their scent, their taste, their vigor. And I remember a time the ball came squirting out of the scrum and was just sitting there, tantalizing, fifteen feet away. Josh jumped up and started toward it. But I grabbed the cuff of his pants and held on.

"Becky, Becky," Josh shouted, "step on his hand!"

My darling daughter did just that, stomping my wrist with a tiny sneaker. But Daddy was tougher than a five-year-old foot. So Josh unsnapped his pants and slithered out of them. I could, of course, have thwarted the move with a mere calf-grab, but it was clever enough to deserve success. Josh cantered across the yard in his underwear, helpless with laughter. I feigned outrage and chased after him waving his jeans wildly over my head. Rebecca couldn't move, convulsed as she was with laughter on the ground.

I RECOMMEND FALLBALL to all Daddies. It's a far more joyful game than baseball or football or basketball, any of those goal-oriented sports. It's free of rules; it is organized only by the urge of young muscles trying themselves out against old ones. It's a perfect Daddy combination of exercise and rest, combining as it does wild chases with immovable piles of people. It's a great game, beyond language, a chaos of squeaks and grunts and giggles, a chance to lose yourself in elemental closeness to your kids.

For me and my kids, fallball was a perfect place. Josh and Rebecca got a chance to work on their muscles, to try out their strength on an affectionate punching bag. And I got a chance to relax. Buried underneath my kids, the world disappeared. In that tangle of arms and legs, I had a chance to think about nothing. Their little fists were a massage, battering away mortgage payments and career dread. I was a Daddy lion with his cubs, at play in the fields of the Lord.

One word of caution: Make sure to try it when the kids are reasonably small—somewhere between five and eight. If the kids get big and strong enough, the game loses much of its charm. Our fallball idyll ended one day when Josh, having reached one hundred pounds, landed on my head, from a height of two feet.

It was a stunning experience. I wouldn't have missed it for the world.

Daddy Gets Humbled

OR

Of Dressing Dracula and Little Tommy Perfect

he smart sliver of my brain knows that fatherhood is not a competition. But I am, after all, an American male. And so I want to know where I stand in the UPI Daddy poll.

By most standards, I am a good-enough parent. I have some inspired moments, some less-impressive days. But there is one standard—alas, a very important one—by which I am clearly among the bottom five.

The Halloween costume standard.

Oh, by the way, just for the record, Jody is a Halloween loser, too. Every year, come the feast of goblins and ghouls, we play the perfect fools *together.*

Now living with the knowledge that you're the world's worst at anything is disheartening all by itself. But fate has given our Halloween humiliation a special tang. How? By putting us right across the street from the parent who is the *best* Halloween costumer to ever live, the Michael Jordan of kid-costuming. Our neighbor, Leslie Berkovits—known sarcastically around here as Little Miss Perfect Mommy Costume Maker—makes us look even worse than we actually are.

Submitted for your consideration: Leslie's creations last year and ours.

Her five-year-old Andrew was Peter Pan. His hand-made costume included a little elfin Peter Pan hat (green felt, gold satin ribbon, festooned with a real Canadian goose feather), little elfin Peter Pan boots (rubber soles/chamois uppers, curled impishly up at the toe), a little green tunic, a little rubber dagger holstered in an elfin scabbard, and a drawstring pouch full of fairy dust, aka sparkling metallic confetti.

Rebecca went trick-or-treating as something we called a "silly guy." We put snow boots on her hands, wrapped an Ace bandage around her tummy, smeared lipstick on her cheeks, and plunked a colander on her head.

Leslie's eight-year-old Daniel was Davy Crockett. He wore buckskin pants with frontier fringe. He had a Kentucky long rifle that Leslie stole from the Smithsonian and a powder horn slung around his shoulder on a leather thong. When he arrived at our house, he poured gunpowder out of it. ("Sand mixed with coffee," Leslie assured us lest we have safety concerns.) And as for his trademark coonskin hat? Well, let's just say that a week before Halloween, I saw a how-to book about trapping on the Berkovits' coffee table.

Josh went door-to-door last year as a combination baseball player/mummy/pirate. He wore a Mets cap, a tangle of tattered "mummy rags" pinned to his sweatshirt, and an eye patch (actually a black checker) held in place by a loop of tape around his head.

"Tell everybody you're a baseball player who got buried alive," Jody said, vamping, "who clawed his way free and decided to get revenge by plundering ships at sea."

Leslie's three-year-old Samantha was Peter Pan's sidekick, Tinkerbelle. She flew from house to house.

Last year was not even an exceptionally bad year for Jody and me. We've had worse. A few of our greatest hits:

The Mad Scientist

This is a three-step "costume." Step one: Lacquer child's hair with enough hair spray so that it stands straight up in Einsteinian fright-wig style. Step two: Hand child a plastic test tube from a chemistry set. Step three: Push child out door; say, "Have a good time, honey."

The Unspecified Ethnic Person

Step one: Tie a colorful piece of fabric around child's head. Step two: Teach child a generic Eastern European accent, like one of the Gabor sisters ("Trick or treat, dahling"). Step three: Push child out door; say, "Have a good time, honey."

The Flapper

Step one: Find a long string of faux pearls. Step two: Give a quick Charleston lesson. Step three: Push child out door; say, "Have a good time, honey."

Those are just the tip of our pathetic iceberg. One year we told Josh he was a wizard, used the mad scientist hairstyle, and added a golf club (four-iron) as a magic staff. We once dusted Rebecca's hair with flour, told her to hunch over and wave her fist, and sent her out there as A Crabby Old Woman. You don't want to know about the vampire nurse.

I'm not sure exactly why we're so bad and Leslie's so good. Yes, it has something to do with sewing skill, but our failings go deeper than that. Somehow Jody and I are always *surprised* by Halloween's arrival. By now the breakfast scene is a family tradition.

The kids are sucking down Frosted Flakes, peeking out the window for the school bus, when one of them will casually say, "Scott's coming trick-or-treating with us."

For a beat, Jody and I just look at each other accusingly as though to say, "You forgot Halloween again?" Then we both jump up and start rummaging through the kitchen cabinets in search of some Tupperware that might be the centerpiece of a robot suit.

Somehow I'm sure the same morning at Leslie's house is very different. I picture her going to the hall closet on Halloween morning, pulling out three gift-wrapped boxes, and making the costume presentations. For Daniel, a complete Ben Franklin—including ruffled shirt, knee britches, and a bolt of lightning. For Andrew, a cowboy costume with home-forged spurs that jingle-jangle-jingle. And for Samantha? How about an Amelia Earhart barnstorming outfit featuring jodphurs, a leather flying cap, and the original sextant from the plane that disappeared without a trace somewhere north of Fiji.

I LIKE TO think there are other, perhaps less showy, parenting skills at which we are better than Leslie. I like to think our virtues as parents are more subtle than mere Halloween haberdashery. I like to think we're doing things for our kids that are just a little more important than some fairy costume. I'm not convinced it's true, but I like to think it.

There is really only one consoling thought: Although Jody and I may well be the worst parentcostumers *currently* in charge of kids, we are not the worst *of all time*. No, that title goes to another mother.

Travel back in time to 1961.

An eight-year-old girl goes off to Brownie meetings without any of the colorful little badges sewn on her uniform. While all the other girls' dresses are frocked with colorful merit badges, spritely troop numbers, the snappy, quasimilitary fruit salad of affiliation and achievement, this little girl's was stark naked, austere, bald, denuded of decoration.

"Plain little brown dress," Jody still mutters in her sleep from time to time. "I looked like a tiny waitress."

Daddy Gets Angry

OR

*Of Pig Sties, Shouting,
and Sigmund Freud*

On countless occasions, I have been absolutely sure that now, finally, I had achieved some fundamental understanding of fatherhood. But inevitably, my "insights" turned out to be mirages. All except one. I have one durable piece of wisdom about fatherhood. I know something important about Dad anger. I learned it over the years, on my daily good-night visits to Josh's room.

Each night, as I started toward the boyo's room, I had nothing more in mind than a few minutes of father-son palaver. My purpose at day's end was just to dovetail our paths for a beat, to be "Taps," a reliable refrain before sleep. Unfortunately, that's not usually how it worked out.

Nine nights out of ten, as soon as I got an eyeful of his room, those sweet Daddy urges gave way to annoyance. No, make that anger. Though on my way down the hall, I had imagined greeting Josh with "Hey, champ," by the time I turned the corner into his room, I was usually barking something like, "Clean up this pig sty, now!"

How do I describe the primordial chaos of Josh's room? A Hurricane Andrew comparison? A ground-zero simile? Whenever I see Josh's room, I expect to look up and see the vice president in a chopper doing a damage-assessment fly-over. Perhaps just a plain catastrophe report speaks most clearly.

The dresser drawers are ripped from their slots and spread out across the floor, their contents scattered in a circular pattern as a result of the blast. In the corner, fanned out like glacial moraine, are the three thousand pieces of the X-Man game. The junk on Josh's desk usually includes half a banana, my crescent wrench, three grand in Monopoly money, a skudgy tank of sea monkeys, several chunks of foam rubber (apparently ripped from his pillow), a soccer shin guard, four comic books, a melon baller, some feathers, and a Pizza Hut promotional cup featuring an inch of week-old orange juice. Hanging over one of the curtain rods, there is often a towel and a sock; over the other, a pair of Jockey shorts and a rubber snake.

The interesting fact about my nightly slide from the sweet guy who started down the hall to the angry one who did the shouting was that I was not in control of my anger. Even though I'd tell myself to chill—this was, after all, just a messy room and an eleven-year-old boy—somehow the sight of the wreckage always overwhelmed my resolve to stay cool.

Don't misunderstand me. I was entitled to be annoyed at Josh. The condition of his room showed a lack of respect for me, his mother, his grandparents, for civilization itself. But my anger didn't fit the crime. It was too big, had a sharpness, a momentum all its own.

Neither was it honest. For a while, I tried to explain it with the standard parent rationalizations for shouting at kids. I was tough on Josh because I had to prepare him for the future, teach him discipline, yadda-yadda-yadda. But this was patently false. At the moment that I got angry I wasn't thinking about the future. I was thinking about what his room looked like *right now.* Besides, I knew that most of the successful, fully equipped men in the world had lived, at age eleven, in rooms precisely like Josh's.

No, my anger had nothing to do with anxiety about teaching Josh virtues. My anger came from somewhere else. One night when I went to his room right after a business phone call that had not turned out the way I'd hoped, I discovered exactly where.

Once again, I started down the hall with love in my heart. I would lick my professional wounds by cuddling for a few moments with my boy. Once again, I steeled myself to accept the mess I would surely see. But once again, Daddy went off. I yelled at Josh in spite of myself.

When I turned and stormed angrily out of his room, I knew with a sudden certainty that I wasn't angry about the room itself. I was angry at yet-another thing I couldn't control. Josh was the living, breathing embodiment of *my own* shortcomings. When I yelled at him about his room, I was really ranting about my own discombobulation, my own lack of attention and discipline that had diminished my career, my marriage, my friendships, not to mention that business deal I had just blown. No question, Josh took the heat for my self-loathing.

One of the strongest messages sent in the direction of the young American male is that he's supposed to be in command of his life. We're supposed to be the captains of our ships. But few of us are. And into that gulf between the male ideal of shaping your world and cantankerous reality sail the innocent children.

I feel it in my bones that too often our kids stand in for the rest of an uncooperative world. I am absolutely sure that a lot of Daddy anger has more to do with unrealized dreams than it does with messy rooms. Trust me. You're not really angry at them. You're angry at somebody else, a Daddy who is a far less distinguished person than he dreamed of being.

Let the record state that I am foursquare behind the idea that kids should straighten up their rooms. There are countless good reasons to insist they do. But as T. S. Eliot wrote, the temptation that is the greatest treason is to do the right deed for the wrong reason.

Make them clean their room. But not because you're full of anger, but because you're full of hope.

Daddy Loves His Car

OR

Of Deductibles and Dependents

Scholars have built careers exploring the importance of cars to the American male. The conventional wisdom is that our car stands for our freedom the way a cowboy's horse stood for his. Whatever the explanation, there is no question: cars are close to our hearts.

Fatherhood wreaks havoc with our car mythology. The dreams on which we came of age—swanky images of Italian sports cars, reconditioned 'Vettes—are replaced by station-wagon realities. Once he's a father, the same guy who imagined himself hairpinning through the Alps in a Lamborghini is driving a minivan very carefully. With fatherhood, a car devolves from a symbol of freedom into the exact opposite, a symbol of the ties that bind.

My Daddy car troubles began early.

WE HAD JUST driven our brand-new Volvo family wagon (Atlantic blue, vinyl interior) off the lot. The kids were euphoric, bouncing around in the back seat, enthusing about everything.

"Dad, is this car really from Sweden?" Josh asked, as though that was just a little too good to be true.

"*Yahvolg,*" I replied in sitcom Swedish.

"Sweden! Yes!" Rebecca said, as though Sweden was as good as it gets.

"Beck," Josh went on, "try the armrest."

In the rear-view mirror, I saw them doing just that, leaning on their elbows, heads together. In one of the high moments of family life, Rebecca christened the car "Bluebelle." Everybody knew instantly the name was a keeper.

As we pulled into the driveway, Josh asked if we could take the kids down the street for a ride.

Then it happened.

As Josh bolted off down the street to get his friends, Rebecca clambered up between the front seats to explore the cockpit. As she did, I leaned to my right and bumped into her. On contact, she dropped a bag of M&M's. Little candy bullets went flying all over my brand-new car. Reader, what happened next actually occurred in slow motion.

The green M&M hit the back of my seat and then the candy pellet flipped end-over-end through the air. I reached out, hoping to grab it, but muffed the play. It hit the stick shift and ricocheted toward the parking brake where it slipped with an eerie precision down into a crack that was exactly the width of an M&M.

I peered down into the crack, saw the Day-Glo green pellet sitting jauntily on top of the Swedish parking brake machinery, and fought back tears. Within twenty-two minutes of taking ownership of the car, it had chocolate in the works.

Over the next few weeks, I tried everything conceivable to retrieve that M&M. I went to a hospital supply store and bought some extralong surgical tweezers. I tried a macho vacuum. I even considered disassembling the emergency brake unit. The Volvo rep just said that would void the warranty.

For weeks, the M&M just sat down there, taunting me. I couldn't stop looking at it. At every stoplight, I'd take a peek. Once in a dream, the candy spoke. "I'm still down here, pally boy," it said. Then the candy laughed.

Jody wasn't very understanding. She kept minimizing what had happened, as though it was no big deal that there was snack food in the emergency brake. She didn't understand. To her, a car was just transportation. To me, and every other self-respecting man in America, a car was something more.

Then one day when I peeked down, the candy was gone. It had vanished. But not, I knew, to some distant place. No, it could only have migrated, or even melted, down deeper into the car. I feared that it could find its way into the carburetor. I wondered if there were a fuel additive that would break down the cocoa bean.

As bad as it was, the M&M was just the opening salvo in the kids' assault on me and my car. Consider the following entries from my diary of car destruction:

> June 7: Josh kicked in rear stereo speaker. Opened door with a heel-first move made popular by federal narcotics agents entering premises uninvited.

> July 24: Kids from down the street crouching behind Bluebelle. Fusillade of small-arms fire whapping into the car. Josh and Rebecca firing chestnuts at their friends. Sixty-eight chestnut-impact craters on the driver's side. Resale value of two-month-old car (original price $17,853.87) now somewhere between $150 and $200.

> August 6: Crayons left on dashboard. 98 ℉. Lime green. I am despairing. Lowest day of my life.

Perhaps no other crime against my car and my car mythology is more revealing than the story of what the kids did to the back seat.

THE FIRST DAY of spring.

All the neighbors were clattering around outside, clearing away fallen winter branches, sweeping off their porches. The air was full of promise, and I was fully equipped—for the annual spring-cleaning of my car, that is. Rags, bucket, sponge, whiskbroom and Dustbuster, furniture polish to make the dashboard gleam.

I waved in howdy to Larry and Paula across the street, crossed to the car, opened the back door, leaned in, and pressed the lever that released the bottom of the back seat. But when I lifted it clear and saw under the seat, I gagged, then staggered backward, whacking my head on the door frame as I drew clear of the car.

Plain decency forbids a detailed description of what I saw under there. But let's just say that apparently, on all those trips when Jody had so lovingly passed food over her shoulder to the kids—to calm their little car-sick tummies—they hadn't been eating it at all. They had been making a compost heap under the seat.

Well this was the last straw. I had had it with the way the kids treated Bluebelle. I sat on the blacktop, stunned by what I had seen, and I swore that the kids would never ride in the car again. Next time we went to visit Aunt Eileen and Uncle Greg, they could arrange their own transportation.

Let's just say that lots of stuff congeals around old half-sucked Lifesavers. And that taco chips, pretzel nuggets, and a melted red crayon ferment into a frightening mass—at least when they are honey-glazed with dried grape soda.

I stood up, took a deep breath, and set to work reclaiming my car. As I worked angrily away, scraping, clawing at glutinous congealed masses of gum and apple cores and Popsicle sticks, I wondered what that green stuff was. And for what possible reason the kids had torn a coloring book into three million pieces. I also worked on my lecture, practicing the peroration the kids were going to get.

That night, I sat down at dinner, all set to deliver my lecture/ultimatum. As Jody brought in our plates, I launched into a good old-fashioned rant-and-rave.

"Kids, there are going to be some changes made about eating in the car," I said. But no sooner did I start to describe the grotesquerie under the seat than Josh and Rebecca looked at me, stricken, as though falsely accused.

We didn't do it, Dad, they said. We're always careful about crumbs. We would never drop Jujubes. We always keep our wrappers in our pockets until we get home. We love Bluebelle, would never treat her so disrespectfully.

"Then who did it?" I countered, caught off-guard, I admit, by their brazenness. "You're the only people who sit back there."

"No, Dad," Josh said seriously, as though determined to get to the bottom of this mystery. "When you and your brothers went to play golf? Uncle Kevin sat in the back."

"Yeah," Rebecca added. "And remember when Mr. Turoff's car broke and we gave him a ride to the train station? He sat back there, too."

I was in awe. These two were cool customers. They looked me right in the eye and denied the whole thing. And not only that. They fingered their uncle and the dentist from across the street who had taken them to three Mets games last summer.

"So you think Uncle Kevin chewed a Mallomar, spit it out, and then wedged it under the seat?" I said.

"He must have," Josh said.

"Or Mr. Turoff," Rebecca added, Sherlock on the case.

I took my plate and ate in my room.

Daddy Knows Dinosaurs

OR

Of Pteranodons and Don Jr.

Statistics show that five out of ten fathers (seven out of ten with sons) will have to navigate the Dinosaur Days, that interlude when dinosaurs are everywhere—etched on backpacks, stenciled on sneakers. And fathers can make a big mistake if they don't get dinosaur-literate. You don't want to be one of those guys who doesn't know his icthyosaur from his saltopus.

Once when Josh was in dinosaur overdrive, he came swooping into the room, vrooming a plastic prehistoric creature. He and his winged companion banked left and landed in my lap. When I referred to the creature as a "dinosaur," he squirmed out of my lap and scooted back into his room.

To a child enraptured with dinosaurs, a father who calls a *pteranodon* (largest flying creature ever) by the generic word "dinosaur" is barely a father at all. It's like calling a shark a "fish." Or Shaquille O'Neal a "basketball player." The kids expect better from the big guy.

And so I set about to educate myself vis-à-vis speciation of the great lizards.

I borrowed his dinosaur books. I studied. I learned. And within a few weeks, I could identify a trachodon at a glance. I could even distinguish *Monoclonius* from *Triceratops*. There were dinosaurs who couldn't do that.

Then one night after dinner, I sashayed into Josh's room, found him refereeing a dinosaur donnybrook, and said casually, "My money's on *Styracosaurus*." I was referring to the many-horned rhinoceros-sort-of-fellow in his left hand. Josh just smiled. Ten seconds later, *Archaeopteryx* bought the farm. Ever since, dinosaur talk has been a shared language, a literacy linking father and son.

So, in the interests of the generations being on the same dinosaur page, herewith a few rudimentary but never-fail Daddy dinosaur memory tips:

> *Brontosaurus:* This is the leviathan, the huge guy with the long neck. Remember the credits to *The Flintstones?* Fred's operating an earth-mover, aka *Brontosaurus*, when he hears the five o'clock whistle and he's out of there. How? Quick. Fast.

Or should I say, "pronto"? Or maybe even "bronto"? Think of the way Fred left work. Pronto = Bronto. It'll help.

Stegosaurus: This is the guy with those triangles running up and down his spine. He looks serrated, doesn't he? Rather like the knife you'd use on a juicy "steg," don't you think?

Pterodactyl: This is the dinosaur that flies. When you see wings, think winged. From winged, go to Shakespeare, from Shakespeare to dactyl, which is a poetic cadence. If you can figure out a way to remember what a dactyl is, you'll remember that the dinosaur with wings—I mean the one who is winged—is named after it.

Tyrannosaurus Rex: This is the guy who stands on two legs and is always baring his teeth. He looks mean enough—don't you agree?—to kill his father and have sex with his mother. Just like that other rex, Oedipus. So, fierce = whack Dad, cuddle Mom = Oedipus = T. Rex.

Now you're ready for the Daddy's dinosaur test.

Dinosaur Matching Test

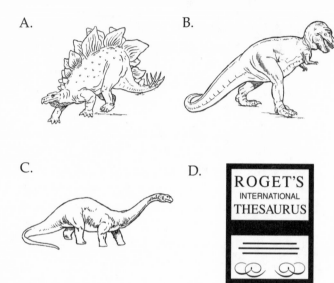

A.

B.

C.

D.

ROGET'S
INTERNATIONAL
THESAURUS

Match the correct pictures and names:

Brontosaurus _____   *Stegosaurus* _____
*Tyrannosaurus*_____   Roget's *Thesaurus* ____

Dad, if you don't—at the very minimum—master these three creatures, use the thesaurus to look up synonyms for "pathetic."

Daddy Takes a Vacation

OR

Of Old Dances and New Hampshire

r. Seuss's classic *Oh, The Places You'll Go* celebrates the invitation known as the world:

> You've got dreams in your head,
> You've got feet in your shoes,
> Unless I'm mistaken,
> You can go where you choose.

The good doctor is unquestionably right—if you don't have children, that is. Often Dad has to go where his *children* choose.

Over the last few months, for example, I've been on the roof searching for the boomerang and on my belly under the house, pleading with a gerbil named Bob. Dad ends up on a few roads less traveled; he sometimes gets to invigorating places.

AS WE ARRIVED at the Happy Hills Resort, darkness fell on the New England hills. Two well-scrubbed college kids in forest green golf shirts greeted us, unloaded our bags, and whooshed us into the lobby and the care of Miss Whitman at the front desk.

"We're the O'Neills," I said.

"Then these," she said, glancing down at a three-by-five card on the counter "must be Josh and Rebecca."

After greetings all round and the surrender of a credit card, she said to the kids, "We've put you in Algonquin Cabin. It's named after a tribe of Indians.

"For your convenience, Mr. O'Neill," Miss Whitman continued, handing me the keys to Algonquin, "any member of your family can charge any of the services at Happy Hills simply by signing their name and their cabin number."

Josh who had been, until then, lolling across an armchair under a moosehead suddenly perked up. "Kids can charge things?" he asked, leaping toward the desk.

"Well, no, Josh," I said, casting Miss Whitman a sidelong help-me-out-here glance. "Only parents can sign for things. Right, Miss Whitman?"

"Actually," Miss Whitman countered, "the children can sign for things too, Mr. O'Neill. In fact, if they run short of quarters at the arcade, we'll advance them a roll without a service charge."

"Awesome," Josh said, turning to Becky and explaining, apparently, that this wasn't New Hampshire, after all, but the promised land. He grabbed some postcards from a rack on the counter, sat down, and started practicing his signature.

"First name *and* last name?" he shouted to Miss Whitman.

"No, last name and cabin number will do," replied our hostess.

"What's our cabin number?" Josh shouted back.

"Never mind—," I began.

"Fourteen," Miss Whitman yelled over my attempt to interrupt.

Miss Whitman and I exchanged glances.

She knew I knew.

And you know what?

The woman didn't care.

I looked over at Josh. He was writing the number *14* over and over again.

"Is that fourteen?" Becky asked him. Josh nodded and offered her a high-five.

"Room service," Miss Whitman spieled on, "is available until midnight simply by dialing extension 42. That's a four and then a two. The menu is on the mantel over the fireplace. You might have to stand on the end table to reach it."

"Pardon me—?"

"Never mind, Mr. O'Neill."

I vowed to talk to somebody in the state attorney general's office.

"Enjoy your stay at the Happy Hills," she said. "Tom and Benjy will show you to your cabin."

We got to Algonquin and settled into our sylvan retreat. After a few minutes of unpacking, the kids tumbled, excited but exhausted, into bed in the other room. Forty minutes later, as Jody and I were about to turn in, I answered an unexpected knock on our door.

Suddenly four guys in mustard-colored waist-length jackets with nametags came charging/clattering into the room, pushing carts in front of them. "Don't be a hero, Hugh," Jody shouted as she slithered, entirely naked, off the bed and into the bathroom. "Just give them what they want."

"Room service for Mr. Josh O'Neill," their leader, Randy, chirped. In a flash, what had been a quiet country cabin exploded into the Oyster Bar at Grand Central. The intruders, who couldn't stop calling me "sir," began moving furniture, making way for a feast.

In a maelstrom of silverware and napkins thwapping open, they set up a dinner of pea soup, shish kebob, and cherries jubilee for four, two of whom were—fortunately for one of them—asleep in the next room. There was also one serving of veal marsala, one fudge brownie with ice cream, and two baked Alaskas.

"For the gentleman," Randy said, waving his hand over the plates, introducing the food, "a lovely baby veal. And for madame," he continued with just a trace of a French accent, "*zee* chicken poached in *zee* pear sauce." With that he swept his SWAT team out of the room.

The door to the bathroom opened and Jody peeked out. She was wrapped in the bedspread.

"Are they gone?" she asked.

I nodded and said, "Room service, compliments of Josh."

"Did you sign anything?" she continued.

I nodded.

"Can we get a loan to cover it?"

"No sweat," I said. "We've got equity in the house."

We hunkered down over the carts and started eating. We sampled this, sampled that. As we sipped and nibbled, we actually talked, had a grown-up, just-us, uninterrupted conversation.

By the time we had polished off the tasty main courses and made a dent in the dessert mountain, our scorn had shifted from Josh to the room service guy who had—on orders from a nine-year-old—sent us enough pounded veal to feed Avignon for a fortnight.

Our middle-of-the-night meal was an odd, unexpected moment of parental privacy—our first in eighteen months. We reminisced, planned, fed each other, traded both deep thoughts and sassy one-liners. We were, my partner and I, dream dinner companions—lighthearted but not frivolous, with champagne wit and sound hearts. We talked about the world currency crisis and Rebecca's third birthday party. Jody was Carole Lombard in a 1940s movie. And I, well, I was one of those guys who played opposite Carole Lombard.

The kids, asleep just behind the door, seemed miles away. And though when we tumbled into bed, we were far too logy from gluttony to try our hands at lust, we were deeply grateful to Josh for the most romantic dinner of our lives.

THAT VACATION WAS everything we needed. The kids went on hayrides and caroused with forty-two other children. Jody and I traded murder mysteries by the pool and slept during the hayrides. But checkout time was no picnic.

When Miss Whitman hit the button on the keyboard to print out the bill, the computer just kept whirring and whacking, spewing pages. I had to drag it over the counter.

As I followed my finger down the column of charges, it was clear that room service was not Josh's only enthusiasm. He had signed for a tennis lesson and seven rolls of quarters at the Ethan Allen Arcade. He had signed for twenty-two bingo cards and the entry fee to the bridge tournament.

"What's this charge?" I asked pointing to an entry coded TNG.

"Oh, Josh took a tango lesson from Rita." she said, turning her head suddenly to the side and taking three quick Argentinian steps. "He's a natural dancer, you know."

"Tango?" I asked.

"Yes," Miss Whitman said with a straight face.

"And what's this charge?" I said, pointing to WLZ, farther down the inglorious column.

"Oh, waltz lesson—discounted," she said. "It was a package with the salsa seminar."

The final entry, corresponding to a chit signed *decjy* was for six rolls of Lifesavers at the gift shop.

"Joshie helped me with my letters," quoth the proud girl.

I just signed and fled.

That night, back home after six hours on the road, as we were unpacking, Jody gestured me over to the door to Josh's room. There, in the half-darkness, our boy was dancing around the room with our girl, bobbing and counting, teaching his sister to waltz.

In another of the small surprises of parenthood, a seed had flowered. Who knew that a dance lesson for a nine-year-old boy—which seemed at the time so annoying, so excessive, such a waste of dough—was actually the bargain of the century?

The kids caught us watching them.

"Becky's great at the tango," Josh said with brotherly pride but no idea they were doing the waltz, "and she never even had a lesson."

Daddy Tees Off

OR

*Of Nicklaus, Palmer, Watson,
and Thoreau*

If James Joyce was right about our errors being portals of discovery, then a miniature golf course—the Poconos Putt-o-Rama—was the door to Saint Basil's Cathedral. I made a honey of a mistake there, and on the eleventh hole (dogleg left, up a ramp, through an alligator to an elevated plywood green) I made one major discovery about children.

IT WAS REBECCA'S sixth birthday. The plan was to simulate the PGA championship: cake and juice and miniature golf for everybody. According to the log at Putt-o-Rama, Jody paid greens fees for eighteen.

Even before we teed off, there were bad omens. The kids battled over who would play with what color ball. Brenda complained that green didn't match her shorts. Julian "hated yellow."

Sensing chaos, I jumped into the breach with parental authority. "Rule number one: Any dispute over the color of your golf ball," I said, choosing order over good cheer, "will result in immediate disqualification."

I looked over at Sean who had Joey in a chokehold with the midget putter.

"Rule number two," I went on, "no player shall at any time hold his club against the trachea of another player."

"What's a *traker?*" Brendan asked.

"It's my neck," Joey gasped.

"Close enough," I said.

While the kids were choosing clubs, Jeffrey claimed to have won the world miniature golf championship. His twin brother, Mark, in an attempt to publicly humiliate his clone, shouted, "He's never even played miniature golf before."

Nice, I thought, very nice.

"Shut up, Mark. I have too played golf."

"Oh, yeah? When?"

"Uh, uh . . . I . . . I . . ." Jeffrey stammered, paralyzed by the fact that he and the Grand Inquisitor not only had identical DNA packages but identical life histories. "I played once when you were asleep."

My heart broke for the little liar.

But before I could even say anything in his defense, Jeff lunged past me and stabbed his brother in the belly

118

with the business end of his putter. When I stepped between them, I took a club head in the kneecap.

I should have enjoyed it more; it was the high point of my day.

On the tee at number one, the first foursome argued about who should tee it up first. I gaily suggested the birthday girl should have the honor and then we go in birthday order. Mark said that was unfair to kids born nine minutes after their stupid-head brother. He teed up his ball in protest. Another boy—Brian, I think— kicked it into a wishing well on the ninth fairway.

I wrapped five or six of the kids in a big old Daddy hug—or was it a threatening headlock?—and gave a quick little speech about how if there were sportsman- ship we would all have a wonderful time. Absent cooperation, I went on, our memories of Becky's birth- day would be full of recrimination.

"Rule number three," I had to announce a few min- utes later, "no player shall help another player count his shots."

"Eleven . . . twelve . . . ," said Jill in gleeful play-by-play on Beth's first dozen strokes.

"Three," Beth chirruped as her ball clunked into the hole.

There was mayhem in the air.

I did a quick count of the children. Came up one short.

"Jode, give me a count, will ya?" I yelled through the clamor to Mom.

"I make us minus one," she shouted back, apparently unconcerned since both of the kids to whom she had given birth were accounted for.

I got frantic. There's nothing I hate more than having to tell a parent I lost a child somewhere on the front nine. "Lock the front gate," I shouted to the kid in charge.

"Hey, I don't do security, pal," he replied. "I do lessons."

I grabbed a perfectly calm little girl—Wendy, I later learned her name was—by her shoulders and said with panic in my voice, "We've got to find somebody."

"Who?" she said.

"I don't know. Who's missing?" I answered.

"I think Jonathan's in the windmill," she said, clearly worried I was exactly the type of man her parents had warned her never to talk to.

I raced across to the windmill and found a little boy cowering inside. He was holding a rather large hunk of devil's food which appeared to have been ripped from the birthday cake we had left in the pro shop "for later."

"Are you with the Becky O'Neill party?" I asked.

"Yes," he confessed, trying to hide the fistfuls of cake behind his back.

By the fifth hole everybody was hitting golf balls simultaneously. Orange and blue and green golf balls were wheering around Putt-o-Rama, like mesons in a particle accelerator. Becky's friend Jessica hit a shot that would have done Tom Kite proud—a low boring liner that ricocheted off Sneezy's foot into Josh's chin.

"Hey, mister, there's a liability ceiling of ten grand," said the teenage manager.

By the tenth hole, kids were actually dueling with their putters. There was dental work in the air.

The kids were no longer playing golf but some variation on hockey, pushing their balls toward the hole, à la Gretzky swooping the puck across the neutral zone. Every one of them claimed to have a hole-in-one on every hole. Believe it or not, when we got to the eleventh hole—the seven-yard dogleg left through the alligator—things got worse.

Brendan, who was—may God hold him in the hollow of his hand—the only child still actually *striking* his ball, rolled a handsome putt up the ramp and cleanly into the alligator's throat. It did not, however, come out the other side.

"Becky's Dad," he said sweetly, "my ball got stucked." He actually appeared to think I could help him, that maybe a grownup knew something a six-year-old didn't. I loved him for that.

I got on my hands and knees and peered down the reptile gullet into darkness. There was no light at the end of this funnel. But I could see Brendan's ball stuck near the papier-mâché reptile larynx.

I stretched out on my stomach across the fairway and reached down the gator's throat. The ball, needless to say, was just out of my reach.

I stretched still more.

I grazed the ball with my fingertips, tried to poke it out the other side. No luck. I strained. I could feel the ball's dimples.

"Can you get it, Becky's Dad?" asked the only child in the world I cared about at all.

"Almost, Brendan . . . ," I croaked.

"Fore," I heard from behind the castle.

Brendan turned at the sound.

A golf ball whizzed past his knee.

And hit my temple with a fleshy clomp.

"Aaarrrgggghhhhh . . . ," I opined, rolling over on my stomach, in the process twisting my arm in the alligator's throat. When I tried to pull it free, I couldn't budge.

"Brendan," I said with fake calm in the manner of Timmy telling Lassie to go get help, "go find Becky's Mommy." I cast a fearful sidelong glance at the tiny foursome up ahead. They could sense weakness. If they knew I was helpless, they'd pounce.

Mark looked back at me, prone and pinned. He smiled a carnivorous smile. He said something to his brother, who turned to look at me but then decided to whack his brother with his putter again. I remember the sound of cast iron against anklebone.

The last thing I remember clearly is Jody arriving at my side. I remember resting my head in her lap.

WHAT WAS THE lesson I learned? Actually, I learned two lessons—one practical, one philosophical.

The practical parent lesson was never to give eighteen six-year-olds clubs, projectiles, and large doses of sugar at the same time.

The philosophical lesson was that children are the opposite of golf. Golf is a liturgy of etiquette and manners. Golf is manicured, refined, and disciplined. Golf is self-control. Children are none of those things. Children are—what's the word?—wild.

"In wildness is the preservation of the world," wrote Thoreau. He never wrote a word about minigolf.

Daddy Is Cold and Very Tired

OR

Of Alchemy and Extra Innings

The headline was simple: METS BEAT CARDS 1-0 IN 17TH INNING. But as always, the story was more complicated. The story was about the alchemy of parenthood, how sometimes children can actually turn dross into gold.

I had promised all season to take the kids to a ball game and hadn't come through. Now it was late September, the Mets were a gagillion games out of first place, playing out the string in a jinxed season. Though football was in the air, I tried a last-minute make-good on my promise. But even as we got in the car, I knew I wasn't in the right mood for a game. I didn't have the joy of a father-kids expedition in my heart. I wanted, more than anything, to stay home.

We arrived at Shea Stadium—seating capacity fifty-six thousand—to find three thousand diehards in the stands. The air was crisp, the sky autumnal blue. Jets from LaGuardia Airport roared overhead. We wandered down to some great seats right behind the dugout.

The kids were buoyant. For Rebecca, it was her first baseball game. She loved the spectacle, the vastness of the place. She loved the giant scoreboard, relaying scores from across baseball America. She loved the ground crew scooting around the infield. She loved the ushers' uniforms. She loved the romance, the brash, epic quality of the near-empty coliseum. Not I. I had seen it all before. I wanted to be home—where Jody was. Home—where it was nice and warm.

Josh, by now an old hand at ball games, was enthused for a specific reason. "We'll get a foul ball for sure, Dad," he said, figuring since there were so few fans the odds of grabbing a souvenir were pretty good. My attitude was best summarized thusly: Big deal. I faked enthusiasm.

As we settled in, bought some hot dogs, peanuts, and pretzels, my mood perked up a bit. There were plenty of worse places to be, I told myself, than behind a dugout eating junk food with your kids. Still, the cranky me was sure I should have brought a heavier coat. The gametime temperature was, let's say, brisk. I pictured Jody in the living room cuddled up with a good book and a cup of chamomile.

The game itself played out uneventfully. Half the players were minor leaguers getting an end-of-season look-see. Absolutely nothing happened. It seemed as though every batter worked his way to a full-count before popping out.

The innings dragged by.

The temperature dropped as they did.

About the fourth inning, I started calculating what time the game would end. If the second half of the game was as long as the first, ten o'clock seemed optimistic. Even as I was watching the clock, Josh and Rebecca were in heaven. They flipped through the yearbook, reading aloud to each other about obscure utility infielders.

They ate some more.

The fifth inning unfolded in slow motion. Every batter stepped out of the box after every pitch and looked around. It was tough to blame them; they were savoring their brief visit to the bigs.

The temperature dropped again.

The game crawled forward. The most exciting thing that happened was when the temperature slid into the twenties. By the time we got to the seventh-inning stretch, half the fans had gone home. This game wasn't a scoreless duel, a cliffhanger in which dominant hurlers were throwing zeros at each other. No, it was a scoreless dud. Those of us still left stood and sang "Take Me Out to the Ball Game" listlessly. Rebecca loved the very *idea* of a traditional seventh-inning song.

"Daddy, you mean they *always* sing this song in the seventh inning?" she said, clearly charmed by the customs of the game.

"Yeah," I said as though the seventh-inning song was just about the stupidest thing I'd ever heard of.

"Josh, they always sing this song in the seventh inning," Rebecca said to her brother, certain that if he had known about this, he surely would have told her.

Somehow it wasn't until the eighth inning that the looming horror dawned on me. If nobody scored soon, I suddenly realized, this game was going into extra innings. And then, absolutely anything could happen. Time itself might actually stop.

In the home half of the ninth, fifteen Mets struck out with the bases loaded. Half of those few fans still remaining started for the exits.

Josh and Rebecca clearly feared that I too would decide to pack it in. So they turned to me together and started to testify as though at a revival meeting. This was the greatest, most exciting, and incredible game they had ever even heard about. They had never had more fun. And there was no better father.

Meanwhile the ambient air temperature was in free fall.

Nineteen degrees.

I thought of Jody again. Only this time, she had moved from the armchair into our bed. She was wearing that flannel nightgown of hers.

For the rest of the game, every seven or eight minutes, one of the kids would turn to me and, just to make sure I wasn't thinking about going home, offer some variation on "Thanks for giving us the greatest experience of our young lives."

In the tenth inning. I pulled my woolen cap down to the bridge of my nose. In the eleventh, I put my hands down inside my pants. Nobody got near scoring.

Then, in the bottom of the twelfth inning (temperature: sixteen), Josh's much-anticipated foul ball came floating our way. He instantly eyeballed its arc, jumped out of his seat, and scooted up the ramp toward it. It actually looked as though he was going to get this ball. There was, after all, nobody else in the stadium.

But suddenly, out of nowhere, there appeared about two dozen fully grown male *Homo sapiens*, moving at warp speed toward the ball. They seemed to materialize from under the archways of the stadium. Half of them were naked from the waist up, clearly warmed by the great god Budweiser. They were whoofing, barking as they raced from all directions toward a collision with my sweet-faced, tender-hearted, All-American, red-haired boy.

I got up and ran toward Josh and what was clearly going to be a brutal battle for the ball. A yahoo in fatigues, who I felt sure had never been anywhere near Camp Lejeune, bolted past me and careened into Josh, sending him reeling. I managed to grab Josh just before he banged into a cast-iron stanchion. He was disappointed, but at least he wasn't unconscious.

In the top of the thirteenth, we bought cocoa. The kids slurped theirs down and compared chocolate mustaches. I didn't drink mine. I stuck my fingers in it. Got a second-degree burn. It felt great.

Then, in the fourteenth inning, there was a *second* seventh-inning stretch. Rebecca was breathless with delight as she sang. "Dad, if it gets to the twenty-first inning," Rebecca said, "will there be a third seventh-inning stretch?" I tried to enjoy the fact that she knew her seven-times table, but I couldn't. The pleasure center of my brain was frozen.

By now, in my imaginings, Jody wasn't wearing her nightgown anymore.

The stadium was nearly empty. It was me, the kids, and a handful of guys who were . . . how shall I say it? . . . *overinvolved* in the game. One guy—mid-forties, wearing cut-off jeans and heavy black boots—had something of an attitude toward the Mets first baseman. I hoped he wasn't armed.

By the Mets half of the fifteenth inning, the game was such a masterpiece of incompetence that one of the fifty-nine fans remaining started the tomahawk chop and chant, the rallying cry made famous by Atlanta Brave fans whose team had dominated the National League for the last few years. It was a masterstroke of New York sarcasm, using a cheer made famous by the fans of a first-rate team to deride the feckless locals.

With nobody out in the bottom of the sixteenth, the winning run got picked off third. An Arctic air mass settled over Flushing Meadow.

Then somehow, in the bottom of the seventeenth, the Mets scored. I'm not sure how it happened. By that time, the ice in my tear ducts had blurred my vision.

The children went berserk with delight as the winning run stumbled home.

As we left the stadium, cruising by ourselves down the stadium ramp into the New York night, Rebecca capered alongside me, bouncing, bobbing, enlivened at 12:30 by what she *thought* she had just seen. Our car was sitting all by itself, like a little toy, in the middle of a huge parking lot. For a moment I wondered how the other sixteen fans were going to get home, but then I realized that in their liquored-up condition they would probably just walk home on the median strip of the Brooklyn-Queens Expressway.

"Daddy," Rebecca said, "I can't believe my first baseball game was so great."

Then a remarkable thing happened. Suddenly I wasn't cold anymore. I wasn't tired either. I didn't miss Jody at all. Looking down into Rebecca's face, I could feel this night entering her memory bank. I could feel time burnishing her recollection. And suddenly I understood that, sometimes, parents have to endure the bad moments to get to the good ones. I realized that the elations and delights of parenthood almost always ambush you, arrive when you least expect it. Suddenly I was delighted to be exactly where I was, racing with my children across an empty parking lot under a New York City moon, waving a hometown banner as autumn came to town.

Daddy Can Sing

OR

The Best Thing About Being Dad

Here's the best thing about having children.

I love to sing. And like most folks, when I'm in the shower, I let 'er rip. I do Sinatra, Springsteen. I have both a Whitney Houston medley and packed-house fantasies. But alas, the fantasies are all I have. I can't sing at all. Back in high school, the music teacher often asked me to sing more softly because I was throwing off the rest of the choir.

Don't try telling that to Rebecca.

The four of us were cruising along in the car, James Taylor on the tape player. When an elegiac song called "The Water Is Wide" began, I joined in with Sweet Baby James. And the truth is with Mudslide Slim as backup, some plaintive violins, and a little orchestration, I held my own.

The car got suddenly quiet, the way a theater does in magic moments. When the song ended, there was an extra beat of that silence and then Rebecca, clearly moved, said through a sniffle, "Daddy, that was beautiful." Clearly, I got credit for it all. Words, music, arrangement, performance.

And now, every time Rebecca and I go anywhere in the car, she pops in that tape and asks me to sing "The Water Is Wide." She doesn't want to hear James Taylor. She wants to hear *me*. When the song is over, she looks at me in this admiring way, as though it's just splendid the world has such talent in it.

Rebecca has lots of wonderful opinions. She also thinks I'm strong, smart, funny, and tall. She makes me feel a little of each. F. Scott Fitzgerald once wrote that the greatest gift was to be perceived exactly the way you wished to be. Hallelujah and God bless her! My daughter thinks Daddy can sing! It's enough to put a man in full voice.

Daddy at Daybreak

OR

Of Good Morning and Good-bye

Breakfast is a Daddy gig.

Each morning, I do more than just prepare breakfast for Josh and Rebecca. I embody the morning meal. I become Ceres, goddess of grain, Elsie, goddess of calcium. As I fill glasses with OJ, I summon the vitamin C spirit of Linus Pauling. I am the source, a torrent of pancakes and cantaloupe. Watch your back, riboflavin and protein coming through!

Many times, Jody has offered to take breakfast duty and let me score an extra hour of sleep. But I have declined because I love the dawn patrol.

The fact is that breakfast has always had a special place in father hearts; it's the man's meal. If you doubt it, just imagine any of the male icons eating; five'll get you fifty he's having breakfast.

Do you imagine a cowboy having a spinach salad at dusk? No, you picture Tex having a slab of bacon and a cup of jo just before saddling up. Do you conjure up a soldier scarfing down a midday tuna-on-rye? No, in your mind's eye, G.I. Joe is having powdered eggs at sunup.

And look at the word most often used to describe breakfast: "hearty." Now that's an adjective—wholesome, energetic, honest. No question, breakfast is the macho feast, the manifest destiny, up-and-at-'em meal of choice for frontier-finding, wealth-building, touchdown-scoring men. Got to have a "hearty" breakfast. We've got a country to finish.

WHAT I LIKE most about giving the kids breakfast is the simplicity of the task. Lots of the long-range objectives of fatherhood are complicated. Making sure the kids have just the right amount of self-esteem requires a subtlety far beyond the reach of mortal men. Other Dad missions—teaching them discipline, skating, manners, and math—can require shrewdness, wit, patience, ingenuity, kindness, any number of real virtues.

But not breakfast.

Breakfast is a no-brainer, sublimely simple. If you can slice a melon and pour juice, you're a breakfast master. If you can whoosh Rice Krispies into a bowl and say, "Here you go, kids," you're all set. All breakfast requires is that you be awake. Barely.

Breakfast is not just easy; it's unambiguous as well. With the fancy obligations of fatherhood it's hard to know how you're doing. It's tough to tell if you've been strict enough or gentle enough, if you've asked too much of your kids or demanded too little. But with breakfast—like sports, the other redoubt of maleness—the result is always clear. You know instantly if you did a good job. If your son leaves the house with a little yolk on his chin, you did beautifully, Dad. If he's got some syrup on his jeans, you did even better.

My breakfast time with Josh and Rebecca is a place for me to feel sure-footed on the slippery slope of parenthood. As the kids wolf down the meal, I can actually picture the nutrients warding off a particular germ, can actually feel their muscles and bones growing as they gobble their Wheaties. And for that time my uncertainties about my job performance disappear in the clatter of spoons and cups, the crunch of flakes. I convince myself that though I may not always be the Father of the Year, though I may yell too much, change the rules too capriciously, if nothing else, I put some blueberries on top of their granola. If nothing else, I made them Dad's Cinnamon Supreme Killer Apple Pancakes.

Breakfast is the launch pad of the day, the place where kids get their minimum daily requirements of niacin and iron and whatever. And childhood is the breakfast of life, the place where they will, with luck, get the joy and energy they'll need out there in the world. At the moment I'm actually slathering some toast with peach preserves, I convince myself that we are giving them a hearty childhood, that Josh and Rebecca will leave our house some years hence with bellies full and fuel to burn.

Daddy Goes Rafting

OR

Of Huck Finn and Another American Boy

When Josh was small, I read to him for a few minutes every night before bed. He liked what he called "confusing" books, by which he meant extravagant, fantastical tales, books in which the plain old rules of life did not apply: the Narnia books and the magic stories of E. Nesbit.

When he suggested *Huckleberry Finn* as our next book, I was both surprised and hesitant. Surprised, because it didn't have the tumble-down-a-rabbit-hole quality he usually preferred. And hesitant, because I remembered enough about the book to know that despite its ebullient tone, *Huck Finn* was not G-rated.

Though Twain's novel has over the years taken on a reputation as a kid classic, it's grown-up stuff, a high-spirited but unflinching story about slavery, brutality, duplicity, the reliable ignorance of people and institutions. It also features some big-league family dysfunction—Huck's dad was the original abusive, alcoholic father—and the racist language of its day.

But Josh had it on his friend's advice that *Huck* was a good book. So, figuring we could always change course if the book seemed inappropriate for his age, I decided to give it a try.

"'You don't know about me,' I began in my best southwest Missouri dialect, "'without you have read a book by the name of *The Adventures of Tom Sawyer*.'"

"I like books where it sounds like somebody's talking," Josh said. When the word "nigger" appeared for the first time a few minutes later, I dropped my Pike County dialect in favor of modern Dad.

"Josh, you know, back when this book is set, African-Americans were slaves. They were bought and sold, allowed no rights, treated like objects. White people called them 'niggers.'"

Josh said nothing. I waited a beat, giving him time to sort out the questions surely roiling through his mind. But still, he said nothing.

"You understand, son?" I asked.

"Yeah," he replied, as though I'd insulted his intelligence. "Keep reading."

Over the next few weeks, we traveled together in nineteenth-century America. I enjoyed playing Huck. His voice is a sound you don't hear much today—

buoyant, affable, colorful, susceptible to life. Little by little, each night my Missouri dialect improved.

Though I worried about the routinization of the word "nigger," which appears throughout the book, I didn't change it. I also remembered enough about the story to know that it was precisely the dehumanizing of the slave Jim that set up the emotional climax of the book.

Josh was enthralled by the adventure. To a city boy whose cautious parents never took their eyes off him, the idea of being out there on the river, making your own way, was intoxicating. Josh loved Huck's ingenuity, his daring. And most important, from the beginning he understood the drama of the book's central moral question: What would Huck do? Would he attend to the quiet commands of his conscience and help Jim escape? Or would he hear the conventional voices and send him back to slavery?

As I was reading the passage in which it appears that Huck's bad angel will prevail—the passage in which Huck decides to write a letter to Miss Watson telling her where Jim is—Josh interrupted.

"Dad, how can Huck send Jim back?" he asked, devastated and disappointed in the boy with whom he had come to identify so strongly.

Peeking ahead a few lines, I held my hand up to him in wait-a-sec and read on: "I got to thinking about our trip down the river; and I see Jim before me all the time: in the day and in the nighttime, sometimes moonlight, sometimes storms, and we a-floating along, talking and singing and laughing—"

"He's not going to send the letter, Dad," Josh said with relief.

No indeed. Not our Huck. In the ultimate moment, Huck overcomes the thousand brutal lessons of the society in which he lives and obeys his moral voice. "I took it [the letter] up and held it in my hand. I was a-trembling, because I'd got to decide, forever, betwixt two things, and I knowed it. I studied a minute, sort of holding my breath, and then says to myself: 'All right, then I'll go to hell'—and tore it up."

"I'd go to hell, too," said Josh, a quaver in his voice.

Now Josh knew that Huck's immortal soul was not at stake. On the contrary, he understood that Huck had done the *right* thing. But his assertion nonetheless was no cheap critique from a modern moral high ground. No, his was a well-earned understanding.

He had firsthand experience with the pressure to conform to the cruel conventions of the mob. He was, after all, in grade school.

The thuggery of elementary school is not, to be sure, the enslavement of a people. But the ruthlessness at its heart—the taunt, the insult, the "dis," the sneer, the elevating of yourself at the expense of others—is surely kin to the mundane brutality slavery required.

Among the singular elations of being Josh's father has been the opportunity to watch him move down the river of his life. Though he lives, alas, in a youth culture where derision is coin of the realm and sarcasm the path to social standing, he has refused to traffic in the nastiness that is commonplace among kids. He has been kind and goodhearted among a tribe that values neither virtue.

Josh has the courage of Huck.

Fatherhood has been an occasion to stand near my son's flame and to witness the emergence of a moral man. Our boy is a daily reminder that despite the many come-hithers of the low road, the easily won approbation of those chuckleheads in town, there is a greater glory in going your own way.

"You feel mighty free and easy and comfortable on a raft," Huck said.

Sometimes, being a father, you feel that way, too.

Daddy Dons a
Big Red Nose

OR

Of Fear, Loathing, and Seltzer Bottles

The hero of John Irving's *World According to Garp* warns his sons when they're swimming to watch out for the under*tow*. But one of the boys thinks Garp said "under*toad*" and so, for years, keeps an eye peeled for a giant frog just waiting to suck him out to sea. The imagined monster becomes a symbol for the many perils of the world.

Fathers knows about the Undertoad. Once you have a child, the world is a dangerous place. For Dad, even a trip to the circus is no mere lark. For Dad, even a clown act is a brush with the dark side.

SOME FRIEND-OF-A-FRIEND fluke had landed us in the best seats in the house—first row, about eight feet from the action. The kids were euphoric.

"Dad, I can smell the dirt," Josh said, stunned that we were not in our customary seats in Row T.

As the leaping dog act exited down the tunnel, the clown act came bursting through a paper hoop bearing its name, "Floppo and Friends."

Floppo went darting across the ring and suddenly flopped—a flurry of arms, legs, and big shoes—to the ground. The kids laughed for all they were worth. Floppo got up, took a step, and collapsed again in a boneless swoon. His *friends* gathered around, helped him up, dusted him off, and sent him strutting—left, right, left, then once again face first into the sawdust. The kids went crazy. They loved the act.

"Watch, Mommy, he's going to fall again," a little boy behind us said as Floppo tried to right himself.

After a dozen pratfalls, each of which got a bigger laugh, Floppo's sidekick, Ringo, announced that they needed volunteers from the audience to help Floppo stand up. Josh looked up at me and tried to form a word. But his tongue was paralyzed by the possibility that he might somehow be part of all this.

I looked up to see Ringo heading right toward us. And before I could say a word, he honked his giant bike horn, reached over the railing, picked up my firstborn, and bore him away toward the center of the ring and the prone Floppo. Josh looked back at me over Ringo's shoulder. Nobody had ever been more excited. Not nobody, not no-how.

I enjoyed his pleasure not at all. All I knew was that a complete stranger—wearing a dented derby, your classic red-ball clown nose, and a giant lipstick smile—had just carried my son away.

My first instinct was to leap the barrier and reclaim my child. But I knew in a flash that wasn't an option. Josh would never forgive me. That would cause a permanent father-son rift. He would get married without inviting me, maybe even win the Nobel Prize without calling the old man. As Ringo receded into the distance carrying the light of my life over his shoulder, I struggled with my anticlown prejudice. Dozens of suspicious questions raced through my mind.

Did this man Ringo—was he even a man?—have roots in the community?

Was Ringo the name on his birth certificate?

Did he even own a pair of normal-sized shoes?

As Josh and Ringo arrived—with four other children chosen from the crowd—alongside the fallen Floppo, I knew with certainty that I could not break Josh's heart. Better he be kidnapped and become a circus boy than have his father betray him.

Out in the ring, the "volunteers" from the audience were trying vainly to hold Floppo up. But Floppo did what Floppo did. Flopped. Okay, Floppo was a genius, a physical comedian of Chaplinesque style. My mind raced out of control.

Had Ringo ever filed a tax return? Did he wear those pants when he *wasn't* working? I flashed on some true-crime television docudrama I had seen about a sociopathic clown who one day just went "off." I wondered if Ringo was only smiling *on the outside?* I imagined trying to describe him to a police sketch artist.

"No, no, the hair was wider . . . and bluer," I would say. "And he had a giant target painted on his backside."

As I watched Floppo swoon and tumble and saw the delight in the faces of the kids, I knew I had to rescue my boy from this man who was giving him such joy. I started to mount the barrier, hopeful that the crowd would think the crazy Daddy was just part of the act. But then, before I could break Josh's heart, I looked up to see him sprinting back toward me.

"Daddy, Floppo said I could be a clown when I grow up," he said.

"That's great, pal," I murmured, holding him close. Fine by me. Just grow up safe. Watch out for the Undertoad.

Daddy Goes Hiking

OR

Of Wild West City and Untamed Hearts

We were standing in a canyon, a stone slash in the earth. With the morning sun oozing through the old-growth forest, this was, in every particular, exactly the tableau I had imagined when I had spread out the hiking maps on the kitchen table a month before. As I looked at Jody and the kids—all three fully equipped with fanny packs and trail snacks—I could actually feel the vulgarities of shopping-mall America falling away. Up ahead of us an arrow of mountain water slipped through a cleft into a pool and then poured, a drape of liquid ice, over the lip of a cairn.

I felt linked to the great American nature lovers—to Emerson and John Muir—to every plain, noble man who had ever drawn strength at the breast of Mother Earth. Gazing at the river, I reached down and stroked Rebecca's hair. As I did, Jody leaned down and kissed

Josh on the top of his head. We caught each other's glance. God was in his heaven.

"Hey, Dad," Josh whined. "How much longer do we have to hike?"

Our vacation compromise with the kids had been simple. In the mornings, we had agreed, we would do what Mom and Dad wanted to do, that is, go on inspiring family hikes through the national forest. And in the afternoons we would do what the kids wanted to do, that is, go to some dumb, overcrowded, money-sucking theme park/water park/sideshow tourist attraction. The deal had worked out perfectly—with one glitch. The kids tended to get preoccupied with how long it was until noon.

"Only three more hours, Joshie," Rebecca said, checking her watch.

"Oooh, look," Jody whispered suddenly, pointing into a grove where a doe and a fawn, their flanks dappled with dawn, nibbled on the undergrowth of Eden. I thought I heard flutes in the bright morning breeze.

Josh checked his sister's watch. "Actually, it's two hours and . . . forty . . . seven minutes," he said, a more skilled subtractor than his sister. They high-fived, sustained through this paradisiacal hike by the knowledge that they would soon be once again safe in some crowded souvenir shop trying to decide between a vulcanized rubber tomahawk and a buckskin bag full of gold.

LIKE ALL FATHERS, I have spent a good chunk of my time in Roadside Attraction America. From Walt Disney World, the apex of kid capitalism, to Uncle Franklin's Petting Zoo and Jam Stand, which featured four ducks, a mangy dog, and two jars of peach preserves, I have followed my kids into hundreds of aquariums, theme parks, and pinball/video emporiums. I've been to a grizzly bear museum, Fantasyland, Galaxyland, the Baseball Hall of Fame, the Basketball Hall of Fame, the Fishing Hall of Fame. I have been to Santa's Workshop in three different states. I've been to four underground caverns, three lost rivers, Frontiertown, the Rappahannock Reptile Farm, and Big Andy's Tiny World. Fatherhood has been a dizzying world-tour of sideshow hucksterism that would have left Barnum breathless. At Storyland, I almost duked it out with a guy dressed like Little Jack Horner.

But of all the stops on the kid carnival circuit, Wild West City turned out to be both the most pathetic and finally the most profound.

THE GIMMICK WAS the Wild West in fifteen acres. Wooden sidewalks, buckboards, livery stable, sheriff's office, dry goods store, outlaws, posses, the whole shootin' match. It didn't exactly work.

We paid a king's ransom to a middle-aged woman dressed like an old codger and walked through the entrance shed out onto Main Street. It looked like the set of a PTA production of *Oklahoma*. Lots of leaning plywood facades held up in back by two-by-four struts. This was no rollicking, rowdy frontier town, no place for fresh starts. No sir. This was one down-at-the-heels outpost. This wasn't *Little House on the Prairie*. It was more like *A Little Valium in the Water Trough*. There was depression in the air. This was a paltry caricature of the legend that had once given our country life. One thing they got right: the dust. This place was mighty dusty, pardner.

Over to the right was the Ole Swimming Hole. It was a stagnant little pond jammed with boats that were—unless I'm mistaken—old propane gas tanks that had been cut in half lengthwise and painted with a tree-bark design. Kids tried to paddle around, but the "pond" was so crowded mostly they just clanged into each other amid a swarm of humungous horseflies.

There was a bank robbery scheduled for three o'clock in the town square. Right on cue, a desperado came racing out of the bank carrying a sack of money. Two problems: First, he didn't look much like Jesse James.

He was wearing a tank top and a Mighty Ducks ball cap. And second, he didn't leap onto a horse to make his getaway. He just ran around the corner and ducked into the employees' lounge. A little blonde girl kept shouting to the sheriff, "He went in there! He went in there!" But the sheriff, who was himself wearing spandex, didn't get all lathered up about hot pursuit. He appeared to be ordering a pizza on a cellular phone.

We tried the Old West bumper boats, an aquatic twist of the bumper-car concept. Nothing wrong with the idea. But the engines were so loud that all four of us suffered temporary hearing loss. And the engine exhaust gathered into a noxious blue cloud that gave me a headache that hung on until well past dinner that night.

Over at the Old West mule ride, the kid in charge, who had a plastic handlebar mustache clipped into his nostrils, appeared to be only semiconscious. He helped Rebecca get on the mule without so much as a "Howdy." Then he turned the mule's head toward its tail, spinning the animal in a slow circle. (Notice I didn't say a small loop around a corral. No, the animal turned around in-place, a mulish dervish on downers. The ride lasted four seconds.) Then the kid gestured weakly toward me, as though to say, "Hey, buddy, take your kid. Ride doesn't last forever." I grabbed Rebecca and fled.

The most interesting thing about Wild West City was that the kids just plain loved it. This was the dreariest place I had ever been. This place had a blacksmith who, instead of heating the horseshoe and then shaping it to fit Old Paint, just kept trying different sizes as though he were a sales guy at Thom McAn.

But the kids just didn't notice how bad this place was. They bounced gaily from the Old West church to the Old West saloon, from the Old West auto rally to Old West minigolf. They petted sheep and chased a few chickens. They were in heaven.

As evening came, Jody and I sat, exhausted, side by side on the dusty sidewalk in front of the assayer's office. We both felt we had entered the Twilight Zone. We just watched the kids caper around. And then, as they put their arms and heads happily through the stocks out in front of the jail, I swear I suddenly began to feel the same sense of tranquility I had felt that morning by the side of that mountain stream.

The children had a burble all their own. They were as urgent and wild and unsullied as any forest. Unlike Mom and Dad, they don't need beauty to feel sublime. They can feel holy anywhere. As the noise and confusion of modern America faded away as surely as it had that morning in the forest, I could feel my pulse, and Jody's too, beating to the elemental rhythm of youth.

What Daddy Knows

OR

It's a Big World, After All

Fathers need to be quick studies. Dad has to instantly absorb info on car seats, croup, origami, and oatmeal, stuff a man without kids simply does not have to master. Dad has to know how to get a tiny stretchy sock on a humid kid foot, how to get a giant frayed shoelace through a teensy little shoelace hole, and how to repair a doll's earring.

Perhaps most important, Dad's got to be flawless with battery taxonomy.

On Carrying Batteries and Losing Your Power

If your kids are between the ages of three and ten, you spend a goodly bite of your cash on batteries. In the O'Neill budget, batteries rank third as a budget item, behind only the mortgage and food. In fact, last

December—thanks to Christmas—batteries even nosed out groceries for the runner-up spot.

Batteries are an unreported national scandal. First, they work for about seven minutes. Second, they cost about a million dollars each. To paraphrase Winston Churchill, never has something so overpriced done so little for so many. Congress ought to look into charges of price-gouging or racketeering.

But no use bellyaching. Fact is, any decent father has to carry batteries on his person at all times. Trust me. Any minute you're going to need a nine-volt or a AA. Even if you popped a fresh battery into Giggles the Clown this morning, I promise you come supper, he'll be short of juice.

Few mistakes are easier to make than bringing home a C-size battery for a D-size toy ape. And, believe me, no sentence is more deflating to a child anticipating a tumbling chimp than, "Oops. Sorry, Becky. These are the wrong size."

So in the interests of making sure those words never have to pass your lips, herewith the first Daddy battery identification chart ever published.

A Father's Guide to Juice

Note: Make a copy of this chart, fold it up, and carry it with you in your wallet. Like your car insurance card and your organ donor card, it's no good to you at home.

AAA are the smallest babies. They are also a paternal red herring—very few kid toys take them. Do not buy these unless your remote control is fading.

AA batteries power most hand-held video games. Handy mnemonic device: The people at AA are *addicted* to booze, fighting the alcohol demons, just as your son is *addicted* to those video games.

C batteries are required for most mechanical creatures who flip over or bang little cymbals together.

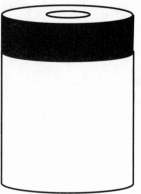

D batteries are required only in the largest toys, like Mr. Olympic's Air Hockey/Football/Croquet Combination Sports Unit. They are *too* big, repeat, *too* big for any doll, including Miss Pinky Tubtime.

 A nine-volt battery is generally required for any toy that does two things at once: the toy whale that breaches *and* sings, the toy oven that bakes *and* broils.

 This is your car battery. Probably dead because your daughter left the car door open overnight again. Call AAA—Automobile Association of America, not to be confused with AAA batteries—and get yourself a jump.

Inquisitive Aside and Warning

Where, one might wonder, are all the B-size batteries?

Please don't ask. Save your energy for cleaning out the basement. Don't drive yourself crazy with questions that have no answer.

Why do salmon fight the current to spawn upstream?

How did Buckner misplay Wilson's grounder in the 1986 Series?

Did Oswald act alone?

Try not to think about the B-size batteries, Dad.

You've got more important things to do.

Daddy Disappoints Santa

OR

Christmas Eve Chaos

Christmas ought to be good Dad terrain. Most men like to see themselves as a slimmed-down version of Santa, a bestower of gifts. Of course, it doesn't always work out exactly the way we plan.

Consider the following poem. It was found behind the top drawer of a roll-top desk bought at an estate sale in the Berkshires. Scrawled on parchment and stained with a few drops of blood (the source of which the poem reveals), it is a withering self-parody, apparently written by Clement Clarke Moore just days after the publication of his more sentimental Christmas poem "A Visit from St. Nicholas." I include it here because it's instructive about the dangerous gulf between paternal myth and Daddy reality.

Dark Night before Christmas

'Twas the night before Christmas, from Currier & Ives
Mom would wrap presents, and I, Dad, would strive
To cobble the gifts, to build, to make ready—
The space lab, the train set, the mechanical teddy.
I'd build them a toyland, we'd dazzle the cuties.
Mom poured the brandy, and I turned to our duties.

At first I was dazzling, snapped A into B,
Linked stanchion to upright, the handyman me.
I breezed through the wagon, pushed wheel onto axle,
With style and a flourish, built a toy *Pteradactyl*.
No plastic could daunt me, no flange or no lever.
I was St. Nick *moderne*, no Scrooge, Ebenezer.
We *kvelled*, meaning beamed, over talking Miss Piggy;
Our spirits were high, our pudding quite figgy.
We were two herald angels, aglow with glad tidings.
The bikes now in pieces they soon would be riding.

But when I got to the fruit stand, the parts in a box,
I started to feel a bit warm in my socks.
I stripped off my footwear, then threw up the sash,
And was back to my labor in a Norm Rockwell flash.
The fruit stand had awnings, it had shelves, it had struts,
It had two hundred pieces, not counting the nuts.
It had tiny bananas, a kiwi, some melons,

It was packed in Bangkok, by some Siamese felons.
But one thing it lacked: there were no directions,
No step-by-step drawings to guide me through sections.

I panicked and forced a small conical part
Down the length of a fruit bin, an ominous start,
Then mistook a side-piece for the fruit stand foundation.
I soon felt the need for another libation.
I twisted and bent, I squeezed, did some thumping;
Within four or five minutes, my temples were jumping.

I used pliers and wrenches—this wasn't much fun—
A corkscrew, some salt, then a soldering gun.
My wife said, "Now dear, take a break. Wanna cuddle?"
"No chance," I retorted, sweat starting to puddle.
The wild in my eye, the cock of my head,
Soon gave her to know she had much to dread.
For the woman I loved had good reason for grievin'—
Of the three kings, her husband had turned into Stephen.

My eyes how they flashed, my forearms how achey,
My blood pressure spoke of that doctor—De Bakey.
More rapid than eagles my spasms they flew,
And up to the rooftops, my curses did too.
It got warmer and warmer, for pieces I searched;
I knew I'd do better sans red flannel shirt.
So off came the garment, then T-shirt beneath,

And annoying Flap L, I chewed off with my teeth.
I started to worry, in the bright Christmas clamor,
When I used my nude arm as a fruit stand Yule hammer.
It hurt not a little, but things got worse still:
I used Barbie's small nail-polished foot as a drill.

My wife spoke not a word, but continued her work;
She filled all the stockings and then turned to her jerk,
"Go up to our bed, oh husband, my dear.
I'll be right up to cuddle; we'll share Christmas cheer."
"This is no time for cozy," from all fours I called.
"I've got to dash away, dash away, dash to the mall,
To find the young kid who said early today,
'I'll build the whole lot for a ten spot, okay?'"

"But dear," said their mother with saintly forbearance,
"The mall is locked up; he's home with his parents."
"His name was Bilecki," I said—no insisted.
"Get the book from the table; I betcha he's listed."

Far from elflike I hunkered, ripping cardboard and plastic;
I inveighed against Christmas, a savage bombastic.
I lambasted eggnog, all this good cheer was stupid,
As were Hasbro and Playskool, even Blitzen and Cupid.
Against Santa himself, I madly blasphemed;
What was so great about sugar-plum dreams?
I spun out of control, a desperate apostle.

What was truth? What was life?
What in God's name was wassail?
I was frantic—a wild man—a creature worth loathing,
Stripped of hope, stripped of words,
Stripped of most of my clothing.

I got back to work, on a bike and a drum
But then closed a hinge on my Christmas Eve thumb.
For an instant in anguish I spoke not a word—
The sound of pa-rum-pum-pum-pum wasn't heard.
But then with my voice I made a great clatter,
And sprang from the rug, so the blood wouldn't spatter.

Somehow the dawn came, and brought Christmas with it.
The bleeding had stopped with the hospital visit.
The kids bounded downstairs and let fly with pleasure.
They felt what, I think, was a joy without measure.
The kids tried the playhouse, they frolicked all through it.
And I don't think they realized just how Daddy blew it.
I don't think they knew it was supposed to have walls,
Or that walkie-talkies were supposed to make calls.
Who cared if the train set only ran in reverse?
"Where are your pants?" had said the night nurse.
The sled it was shaky; my word, how it wobbled.
The hobby horse hobbied but seemed somehow hobbled.
The children went wild, nonetheless, with Yule glee;
I staggered upstairs, found some salve for my knee.

I crawled to my bed, all alone out of danger.
And thought of a child away in a manger.
I thought of a new world, redemption, a Savior.
I thought of my night of psychotic behavior.
I thanked the Lord softly that all was so well,
That the children were hardy this *Joyeux Noel*.
My heart, full of longing, inclined to a poem.
I was humbled, exhausted, completely at home.

The sound of two kids going gaily berserk
Soon gave me to know we had done some good work.
My wife came to see me and sweet-kissed my brow.
She forgave me the fate of the motorized cow.
And I heard my love whisper as she walked out the door,
"Merry Christmas, my fool"; sorry, Clement Clarke Moore.

Daddy Goes to School

Of Miss McGillicuddy and My Team

We hear a lot about the psychological gauntlet that kids go through when they start school. But nobody ever tells you about how difficult school is for *parents.* Especially fathers. For me, from the day Josh started school, I have been locked in a struggle between society—meaning the set of conformist expectations visited on children—and my enthusiasm for my kids.

Parent-teacher conferences have always been a particularly tough event. Though I am, in theory at least, interested in an objective opinion about my kids, I get impatient with anything less than raves. To me, any teacher who is not flat-out delighted by the opportunity to be in the company of my kids is a bureaucrat who has been to one too many conferences on pedagogy.

Jody says that I have some deep-seated insecurity that causes me to take any minor criticism of the kids as a personal attack. And though she says she no longer believes she can help me and I should make an appointment with a professional, she hasn't given up trying to manage my behavior. Indeed, in the weeks leading up to a conference with Miss McGillicuddy, she had a few suggestions.

"Hugh," Jody said one evening as we were doing the dishes, "please, I beg you, no speeches on the glorious diversity of the human soul."

She was referring, I believe, to some thoughts I had shared some years ago with Josh's first-grade teacher.

"And please, no quotes from Emerson or Buddha. Remember, Miss McGillicuddy just wants the best for Josh. She didn't go into teaching for the money."

"Mussolini wasn't in it for the dough, either," I replied, frankly flabbergasted that a woman of Jody's sophistication could swallow the underpaid-dedicated-to-children teacher routine. "She just wants him to behave, get in line, toe the mark," I said. "That's all any of them want."

"Hugh, Hugh, Hugh!" Jody said, shaking me by the shoulders, "Miss McGillicuddy is not the enemy."

That's when she came up with a triple-arm-pat signal. "If it feels to me like you're on the verge of some ranting speech," she said, "I'll tap your arm three times and you'll take a time-out. Okay?"

WHEN THE BIG night arrived, Miss McGillicuddy was wearing one of those old-fashioned, flowered teacher-dresses. She was trying to look all sweet, as though she liked children. I wasn't buying it. Five minutes into the parent-teacher conference, I wanted her behind bars.

"Josh doesn't do as well as he might in group activities," she said.

Oh yeah? I thought to myself, trying to shift angrily in my teeny little grade-school chair. Sez who?

Jody, sensing my attitude, reached over and gave me the triple pat, as though I were a hyperactive golden retriever.

"He doesn't understand the rules of cooperation," Miss McGillicuddy continued.

Oh yeah? I thought. Well, maybe cooperation is for kids who can't go it alone.

"Exactly what do you mean by 'cooperation'?" I asked, as though it were possible to be confused by her sentence. What gives you the right, I was thinking, to criticize Josh?

I think she, like Jody, picked up a little attitude from me. But before she could even answer my hostile rhetorical question, in a flash I knew the answer to the question I had only *thought*. I had given her the right to criticize Josh. Simply by coming to this meeting and sitting docilely in one of those itsy-bitsy chairs, I had given her—and the educational establishment for which she was a stooge—the authority to have at our boy.

Jody gave me another triple arm-pat.

"Would you two excuse me just a sec?" I said, standing up and heading for the door, as though I were going to feed the parking meter.

"Go ahead. Don't wait for me," I continued through a fake smile and with a little wave.

When I got out into the hallway, I turned the corner and quickly flattened myself against the wall, like a television cop in the gun-drawn, about-to-kick-down-the-door position. I startled our neighbor who was sitting in the hallway, waiting her turn to hear her child slandered.

"Sorry, Janet," I said.

"Something wrong, Hugh?" she asked.

"No, no, everything's fine," I replied, tilting my head into eavesdropping position.

I could only hear snatches of Jody's conversation with Miss M.

". . . some difficulty with addition."

So what? I thought. Einstein couldn't add until he was twenty-seven; then he reinvented the world.

". . . occasionally he writes his letters backwards."

"Big deal, Faulkner was dyslexic," I muttered. "Tell it to the Nobel Prize committee."

"Pardon me, Hugh?" Janet said.

"Nothing," I responded impatiently, straining to hear.

Pressed up against the wall like a commando, I decided we were going to take the kids out of that damn school and teach them at home. Jody and I would pass on what we knew of literature and math. We'd teach them about American democracy, about gravity. Most important, we'd teach them to shine their own light. We'd save them from the conformist boot heel of public education.

The pluses of The O'Neill School seemed inarguable. At The O'Neill School we'd educate their hearts *and* their minds. At The O'Neill School, Josh and Rebecca wouldn't have to endure the schoolyard taunts of seven-year-old sociopaths. At The O'Neill School, we'd feed them nutritious hot lunches: whole-grain bread and navy bean soup, not lime Jell-O in a pleated paper cup.

As I strained to hear Miss McGillicuddy's voice, I considered taking our secession even further. We'd withdraw not just from P.S. 6 but from society itself. We'd buy some land, raise our own food, study animal husbandry. We'd have four more children to help with the harvest. We'd buy goats. Every now and then we'd take the buckboard into town for supplies. Even as I wondered if I could single-handedly install solar-heating panels, Miss McGillicuddy nattered on. I picked up fragments here and there.

". . . the phys ed teacher says you might want to help Josh with his motor skills."

You've got to be kidding! Michael Jordan couldn't even walk until he was nineteen!

"Josh often punches children who say hello to him," she droned on and on and on and on.

In some ways the most dispiriting aspect of the whole scene was Jody's passivity. Throughout the tirade against our son, Jody never once raised her voice in his defense. Never took up for the boy. She never mentioned the color of his eyes, the sound of his laughter. She never mentioned how gentle he was with his little sister. No, she just sat there and listened to a woman in an out-of-date dress itemize his short-comings. Made me wonder what calumnies about *me* went unrefuted.

Finally, Jody stood up, shook hands in farewell with Miss McGillicuddy. When she came out the door, I grabbed her by the arm and said, "So what else did Miss Priss have to say?"

"She said and I quote, 'It's the highlight of my life to have spent even one moment in the same time zone as your son,'" Jody said.

"Really?" I said, beaming as we walked down the stairs, past the shin-high water fountains. "What else?"

"She said her only regret is that Josh is so brilliant she can't keep him back a grade and spend another year in the radiance of his sweetness."

"That's a nice phrase—'radiance of his sweetness.' Anything else? Tell me everything," I said.

"She said that Josh must have some dazzling parents to be such a glorious child."

I wanted to believe. So I did.

As we walked out through the gym door into the cool, clear night, I felt myself welling up with relief that finally someone had seen my kids clearly.

Daddy Loses His Dignity

OR

Of Pride and Pediatrics

Before I had children, I liked to believe that I moved through the world adroitly, maybe even—in my best moments—with some grace. And for the first few years of fatherhood, I struggled to maintain my dignity.

But no more. I've given up. The charade has become a joke. Every day fathers are driven into situations that are miles beneath our dignity.

I once chased a runaway puppy into my neighbors' yard and suddenly realized that not only had I interrupted their daughter's engagement party but that I was wearing nothing but a pair of boxer shorts that said "World's Greatest Dad."

"New bathing suit," I chirped to the bride-to-be, trying to pretend I wasn't in my Skivvies. I picked up the pup and beat my retreat.

But even that wasn't the worst of it. No, the most indecorous father moment was yet to come. One winter morning in a pediatrician's waiting room, my male swagger was torn to tatters by paternity.

REBECCA, THEN FOUR years old, had a 9:45 appointment with the kindly Dr. Sonnenfeld. And there was, to my surprise, no complaint about going. She presented herself front and center, fully dressed. No, check that, she was more than dressed; she was positively quilted, decked out in a puffy down coat, a woolen ski cap, *Little Mermaid* mittens, a *101 Dalmatians* scarf, and some Rudolf Nureyev legwarmers. I grabbed my coat and we headed out into the snow-fall.

When we got to the doctor's office, I started to unwrap Rebecca, whipping off her hat and scarf as she worked on her zipper.

"My zipper's stuck, Daddy," she said.

I reached over to help her, drew the zipper down without a hitch, and got something of a surprise—a completely naked child underneath. I flashed back to the obstetrician's first words, "It's a girl."

Under her coat, Rebecca had on legwarmers and snow boots. That's it. She was otherwise thoroughly nude.

"Oh my God . . . ," I gasped as I quickly closed her coat and surveyed the other parents and kids in the waiting room. Nobody had noticed. Yet.

Rebecca cracked up.

"Rebecca, what . . . ," I began. "Oh no . . . ," I concluded.

Rebecca meanwhile was convulsed with leprechaun laughter, actually rolling on the floor, helpless with mirth.

"Daddy, I don't even have—" she began. In a light-speed flash of improvisation, I faked a big manly cough to cover her voice. I managed to drown out the word "panties."

My mind was racing. I had taken a child out of the house without clothing.

In February.

In the snow.

I thought I remembered hearing something on the news about a law that required doctors to report such things to "the proper authorities." Would the kindly Dr. Sonnenfeld drop the dime on me?

I took one more furtive glance around the waiting room. Nobody had gotten an eyeful. So I zipped up her coat, preparing to make a getaway. At least missing a doctor's appointment didn't violate the criminal code. It would be far easier to apologize to the doctor than explain to Jody why Rebecca was spending the night with the people at Social Services.

But as we were heading for the door, the doctor appeared, greeted us heartily, and directed, "Examining Room A. Just take off her shirt and we'll give her chest a listen."

Rebecca laughed.

Jesus wept.

"Sure thing, Doc," I said, in that moment absolutely convinced that calling someone "Doc" proved that you were totally relaxed with nothing at all to hid.

Once inside the examining room, I took everything off Rebecca and sat her on the examining table. Better the doctor think I misunderstood his instructions than know the truth.

When he arrived, I called him "Doc" seven times in the span of three minutes, gave him a quickie update on her cold symptoms, and fled to the waiting room. Actually, I skulked at the end of the hallway, peeking in as he examined her.

After a few minutes, he looked out the door and I strode manfully toward him down the hall, carrying Rebecca's boots, coat, legwarmers, etc., which clearly had her pants, shirt, etc., wrapped up inside.

"How's she doin', Doc?" I said. Dropping the *g* on *doing,* you see, also showed me to be an unaffected, down-to-earth, honest person.

"She's fine," he said. "The amoxicillin is working on that infection. Finish the prescription—that'll do it."

Looking into the man's sweet face, I thought for a moment about confessing. We'd both share a good laugh about the high jinks of raising kids. But I decided against it. After all, the man had legal obligations to the state of New York. I packed Rebecca into her coat, swept her out the door, hailed a cab, and headed home.

"Daddy," Rebecca said, "I told Doctor S. about the trick I played on you."

"Did he laugh?" I asked.

"He went like this," she said, imitating a furrowed doctor brow.

For a couple of days I thought about switching pediatricians. It was hard to see myself taking the kids back there and chatting with Dr. Sonnenfeld as though nothing has changed, as though he didn't know that I had brought my daughter out in a blizzard in her birthday suit, as though he could possibly still see me as a responsible human being. I even called a few friends for referrals. But this man was a terrific doctor. So I settled on a compromise.

Jody took over on the doctor visits.

"Dr. Sonnenfeld sends his best," she said one day after a checkup.

"What did he say, *exactly?*" I asked, nervously.

"He said, 'Give your husband my best,'" Jody answered.

"Were those his actual words?"

"I think so . . . yeah," she said. "Why?"

"Never mind," I said, heading for no apparent reason into the basement.

CALLING ON MY indomitable ability to find the upside of any situation, I actually found a positive spin for even the ignominy of that visit to the doctor. Consider the wisdom of Kris Kristofferson: "Freedom's just another word for nothing left to lose."

Well, once the naked-child episode happened, this Daddy had nothing left to lose. I can no longer even delude myself into believing that I am in command of my life. No. I'm the man who forgot to dress his daughter.

This Daddy ain't got nothin'.

So this Daddy's got nothin' left to lose.

This Daddy is feeling free.

Daddy Stops Shopping

OR

Household Hints from Hugh

he longer I'm a parent, the less I know for sure about raising kids. In fact, after ten years I find myself reduced to only four parental verities. And they're not swanky philosophical principles along the lines of "Beauty is truth, truth beauty." Nope. The sum of my Daddy knowledge is four consumer warnings:

Don't ever buy a boomerang.

Don't ever buy a chemistry set.

Don't ever buy walkie-talkies.

And most important of all, don't ever, ever, ever, ever, ever spend any of your money on a tetherball set.

BOOMERANGS ARE ON sale everywhere in Dad World. The Baseball Hall of Fame in Cooperstown sells Five Hundred Homer Club boomerangs. The souvenir shop at Frontierland sells boomerangs with an Alamo

theme. Boomerangs inscribed with "Come back soon" are piled high in tourist-trap gift shops from Fargo to Fort Lauderdale.

Don't ever buy one. Here's what happens if you do: Your son will throw it. It will not return to him but fall to the ground across the yard. He will think he must have thrown it wrong, so he'll throw it harder, and this time with a little wrist-action. Once again, it will whoot-whoot-whoot across the yard, this time landing four feet to the left of throw number one. He will be—quite wrongly—encouraged. "Did you see, Dad? It was starting to turn." He will then throw the damn thing progressively harder and with more wrist-action until it shatters the window on the side porch.

Fact: Boomerangs do not come back. They are an Australian practical joke on Americans. Don't buy one. If you want something that comes back, go yo-yo. The string works wonders.

All parents want their kids to like science. Why? Because that's where the jobs are. And on your travels through toy stores, you'll see the phrase "including over two hundred experiments" and convince yourself this chemistry set will make little Janey curious about the molecular structure of matter.

Wrong. Nobody's career path has ever been changed for the better by owning a chemistry set. Only two things will be changed: (1) The dining room table will feature a greenish stain that's tough to cover with a doily and (2) the tips of your fingers will have a permanent blue tinge from the time you flicked a plastic test tube with your index finger shouting, "Turn blue, dammit, turn blue."

I have spent close to seven million dollars on walkie-talkies. And learned one thing. They don't work. Even the expensive ones, marketed by companies that ought to know something about communications technology—the name AT&T ring a bell?—do not work. Or, even worse, they work just well enough to send messages like this: ". . . me . . . er . . . by . . . syth . . . so we c . . . apt . . . Mike . . . air." Further, no child has ever mastered the knack of pressing the button down to talk and letting it up to listen. Inevitably, three hours after you buy walkie-talkies for the kids, you'll find one abandoned by the front steps, the other one in pieces in the sink. It's a fitting destiny.

Tetherball is the most dangerous purchase of all. Okay, there's this pole. And attached to this pole is this rope. Attached to this rope is this ball. Two kids stand on opposite sides of the pole and each tries to whack the ball in his assigned direction, so that the rope connecting the ball to the pole wraps completely around the pole. That's tetherball. It is, no question, the heavyweight champ of bad buys.

When Child Number One serves the ball, one of three things, all bad, can happen: (1) Child Number Two can jump up over and over again trying to stop the ball, never laying a finger on it, (2) Child Number

Two can get hit in the face with the ball, or (3) Child Number Two can have the rope wrap around his wrists causing nasty abrasions that will require anti-sepsis and a gauze wrap.

The game is always over in six to twelve seconds and is both joyless for the winner and completely humiliating for the other guy. Clearly, tetherball was invented by some misanthrope who was so depressed he didn't even have the energy to chase the ball. ("Let's tie it to the pole.")

Tetherball is also anathema if you've got long-term wealth-building in mind. A professional real estate association has estimated that in major metropolitan suburbs a fifteen-foot circle of grassless hardpan around a rusty pole and a deflated ball hanging from a string can lop as much as twenty-five thousand dollars off the sale price of a three-bedroom, center-hall colonial.

True, a potential buyer could just take it down. But the mere sight of a tetherball set sends a potential buyer into a low-grade depression. So rather than talking turkey about financing, he'll just slink back to his car.

IT'S NOT JUST that these four items drain the family coffers pointlessly. *That* list of parental "don't buys" has four *thousand* entries. No. These four items are worse than merely impoverishing; they suck the gumption out of a man. And Dads need all the gumption they can muster.

Daddy Loses Consciousness

OR

Of Jellybean Epics and Glassy Eyes

Psychologists who've studied the conversational styles of men and women agree on just one gender distinction. Women enjoy the aimless burble of talk, while men tend to see conversation as goal-oriented—as in, "What's your point, pal?"

Maybe. Maybe not. I don't know. But I do know that any male-female rift is nothing compared to the conversational Grand Canyon between men and kids. Conversationally speaking, men and kids are so far apart no psychologist has ever had the guts to study the gap.

Consider: Men are the strong, silent type. Kids are the small, chatty type. Men cut to the chase. Bingbang. Speak your piece. Lose the palaver. Kids never met a tedious detail they didn't like. They don't know you're supposed to skip the boring parts. Their stories go all around the cobbler's bench or the mulberry bush, whichever way's longest.

Nobody likes to admit it, but for most Dads listening to kid stories is an agony. We all have this idealized image of Dads savoring sweet chats with the children. But the truth is, in the middle of endless kid epics, most men can actually see the sands slipping—one at a time—through the hourglass of their lives.

Over the years, I've tried to follow kid stories that made the *Odyssey* look like a one-liner, stories so slow and serpentine that I wanted to cry out, "Wrap it up! What the hell happened to the bunny?" Not only did my eyes glaze over, my higher brain function glazed over, too. Once, while listening to Rebecca tell me a story about how she found three pennies and two nickels in her backpack and then Brian took one of the pennies and ran down the hall, I actually slipped into a quasicoma.

For a long time I felt guilty about my feelings. I was pretty sure it couldn't help a child's self-esteem for Dad to drift off during the story of Daniel and the raisins and how Blair tried to tie her shoe but wouldn't share her snack with Kate who hurt her hand and then did her homework with David's pencil. But then one afternoon I saw the light and realized there was no reason to feel guilty.

Josh and I were driving around town on errands when, with great enthusiasm, he started to describe an episode of *The Dick Van Dyke Show* he had seen last night. Actually, he didn't start to describe it, he started to recite the entire shooting script. ("Then Sally said to Buddy . . .") When I told him that I had seen the episode back in 1965 when I was his age, he merely said, "That's okay, Dad," and plunged ahead.

Clearly he didn't care if the story was interesting to me or not; he just wanted an audience for his spritz. He continued happily through every twist and turn of the plot ("Then Laura said, 'Oh, Rob . . .'"). At least twice I made it perfectly clear that I remembered the plot of the episode. He didn't care. He nattered on.

That's when I saw the truth. I knew in a flash that his stories weren't supposed to interest or amuse or edify *me*. No, they were supposed to interest or amuse or edify *him*. Somehow, recapitulating a television show helped him shape his experience of it.

I don't presume to understand the psychological kick of telling a story that's boring your audience to death. But one thing was perfectly clear: As long as I was willing to sit there and play the role of audience, Josh was happy. I didn't have to actually pay attention. I just had to give him cover, be a warm body to whom he might conceivably be talking.

Since that day I have been a far-better father. Now, when the kids come bursting through the front door, full of tedious reports about Freddie's Marlins cap falling on the floor and getting all dusty, I don't even try to actively listen. I just turn into a conversational tennis wall. I nod a lot, use the words "great," "cool," the phrase "way to go." For the most part, I just throttle down and let them shower me with mind-numbing gab. I grunt, mutter, chuckle just enough to let them know I'm still alive.

They know I'm not really listening. And you know what? They don't care. In fact, it's fine by them. They may even prefer it that way. Now I can save my listening energy for those times when they actually need my attention, when their hearts are fearful or their feelings are hurt. I can save my Dad attention for those times when it helps to have a grownup hear what's on your mind.

LET'S FACE IT, men and kids are opposites. Men insist that things make sense. For better or worse, we're a cause-effect bunch. Not kids. They don't see conversations or life as purposeful. They don't move in straight lines. They think and act in ways that confound your average logical male.

And what's worse, they make fun of us for being commonsensical. Consider this derision from their hero, *The Little Prince:* "Grown-ups love figures. When you tell them you have made a new friend, they never ask you any questions about essential matters. They never say to you, 'What does his voice sound like?' or, 'Does he collect butterflies?' Instead, they demand, 'How old is he? How many brothers does he have?'"

The point is that kids set out from day one to dismantle the logical man you have spent a lifetime becoming. I'd love to suggest you take a hard line here, stand by the idea of coherence, of making sense. Only one problem with that position. The guys who enjoy fatherhood are the guys who don't.

The guys who enjoy fatherhood surrender. Like a suspension bridge that sways in the wind to survive the storm, they go along to get along. They go with the childish flow, give up the need to understand in favor of an apprehension that is, in truth, deeper and, finally, more satisfying.

Just let the river of these kids wash over you. Don't resist the river, and don't try to figure the river out.

The Daddy in Winter

OR

Of Cocoa and Co-Dependency

Among my favorite intrigues of being Dad is the partnership with Mom. The obligations of parenthood tie Jody and me together in ways that just being he and she couldn't. The child-care conspiracy is a stew of gratitude, blame, teamwork, and the sometimes sick symbiosis psychiatrists call "co-dependency." In fact, sometimes, it's hard to tell where you leave off and your parenting partner begins.

Witness the story of a mother's obsession for which a father paid the price.

ALL PARENTS HAVE fantasy scenes in their heads, idyllic tableaux we dream of assembling for our kids. Jody's fantasy can be best described as The Robert-Frost-New-England-Winter-Day-Snow-Sled-and-Cocoa Scenario. The dream took root early. Within months of Josh's birth in midtown Manhattan, Jody was looking forward to his spending the day sledding in rural Vermont.

"I can just see him *traipsing* into the mudroom, banging the snow off his boots, and asking for cocoa," she said to me one August afternoon on the subway platform at Times Square.

Please understand—Josh was ten weeks old. More to the point, not only didn't we have a mudroom, we didn't have a second bedroom. We lived in a tiny apartment in New York City, which is not the tobogganing capital of the northeast corridor.

But that didn't stop Jody's rural sledding fantasy. A couple of times when Josh was a toddler, we tried to make her vision come true in Central Park. When it didn't work, Jody blamed "the city." But I think the day fell short because Josh just wasn't big enough to *traipse* properly. Or for that matter, to speak.

By the time Rebecca was born, Jody's winter fantasy had become an obsession. A second child somehow quadrupled the power of her imaginings.

We moved to the suburbs.

Why?

They had snow there.

"Hi, I'm your new neighbor," my wife said, greeting the Berkovits family next door. "Where do the kids around here go sledding?"

It was July.

Later that day, as we were driving around our new town getting supplies, Jody pointed to a hill next to the middle school.

"Josh will help Rebecca pull her sled to the top," she said. "And you know what else?"

"No. What else?" I answered.

"They'll *traipse* home together," she said, shivering with delight.

Five months later, about two weeks after Christmas, we got the first snowfall of the year. And Jody's fantasy, nurtured through the city years and summer swelter, was suddenly within her grasp.

She rousted the kids out of bed and told them they were going to spend the entire day—and I quote—"sledding *with Daddy*." Apparently Daddy was to preside over Mommy's fantasy. *I* was to don mittens, boots, earmuffs, go out in the blizzard, and make Jody's dream come true.

The kids begged to go back to sleep.

"Up like a pup," Jody chirped, tossing brand-new snowsuits on top of the lumps under the covers. "No time to dream and drift. *Traipsing* to do."

"So, Jode," I said, "am I to understand that *Daddy* is going out in the snow and Mommy is staying inside where it's warm?"

"Yes," she replied. "You get to *traipse* home."

"And this is a lucky thing for me? To go out in that?" I said with what I can only call a rhetorical Yiddish tone as I gestured toward the Jack London novel outside.

"Yes, you get to hear their joyful shouts," she said, tossing me a ski mask.

"Come with us," I suggested, tossing it back.

"No, Hugh, I can't," she explained. "The mother's supposed to have the cocoa ready when you get home." This from the liberated woman who had said she'd sooner change her name to Betty Boop than take mine when we got married.

"Jody, sledding has nothing to do with gender," I replied.

"Sure, it does," she said, pulling what appeared to be a gingham apron over her head.

"Where did you get that?" I asked, referring to the Pepperidge Farm frock.

"Oh, this?" she asked innocently, as though she had actually at some previous point in her life had an apron on her body. "I've had this for years."

"Gimme the apron," I demanded. "I'll make the cocoa. You go with the kids."

"Do this for me, Hugh," she purred, wrapping her arms around my neck and kind of sqwudging her hips, through the apron, against mine. "It's been my dream."

196

Though I couldn't be sure because it had never happened before, I think my wife was using her body to manipulate me. I think that sqwudge was a promise. Some desperate spirit had taken over my wife. She was Betty Crocker offering a swap. This woman would deliver more than a bundt cake to the man who would make her dream come true.

"Now, go," she said, handing me some mittens and guiding the three of us out into the arctic storm. "Sleds are in the garage—fresh air, full lungs, Norman Rockwell. I'll have hearty treats for you on your return."

"'Hearty treats?'" I inquired with masterful mockery.

She smiled.

"'On our return?'" I mocked on.

"On your return," she said, as though this were a perfectly normal way to speak. "I've got the little baby marshmallows," she went on, beaming from the doorway as we made our way into the whiteness.

It turned out that Jody's fantasy was very much worth having. True, I was extremely cold. Within twenty minutes, I couldn't feel my feet. But bottom line, the children did frolic in the snowfields of the Lord. They squealed and slid and trudged up the hill. Their breath puffed frosty and fresh and innocent. After a couple of hours, the three of us—frozen, weary,

invigorated, towing a sled and a flying saucer—
traipsed home.

Jody greeted us at the door. You could barely make
out the apron behind her smile.

"There's my gang," she said, wiping her hands in
the apron like Lassie's mother, "*traipsing* home
through the snow."

"Mom, it was awesome!" Josh cried.

"Was it, baby?" she replied with rhetorical glee,
beaming at me as she bent to unzip his jacket.

"Josh helped me up the hill," Rebecca added.

"Who needs a mudroom?" she said to me, wiping a
tear with the hem of her apron. "Okay, cocoa all
round," she trilled.

The kids and I sat and sipped cocoa as Jody bounced
around the kitchen offering us marshmallows.

"Did you go fast, Rebecca?" she asked, launching
midget marshmallows into the child's toddy.

Rebecca just nodded as she sipped. "I went on the
sled on top of Josh," she continued through a hot
chocolate mustache.

"Mom, this cocoa is great," Josh piped in.

"Thanks, Joshie," she said, pulling three candy
canes out of her apron pocket and dropping them in
our mugs. "And thank *you*," she whispered to me,
kissing me on the neck.

Jody's New England sledding fantasy had been
achieved. The frosty bucolic dream that she had kept

alive through those slushy urban winters had actually happened. Not in some scaled-down, compromised version.

No.

Fully blown.

In every particular.

Exactly the way she had imagined it.

Later that night, after the sledding duo had gone to bed, Jody asked me for more details of the hillside scene.

"Did they look all healthy and vigorous?" she asked.

I gave her a selfish, quick answer: "Yes, extremely healthy, extremely vigorous." She was crushed.

"Sorry," I said. "But my lips are still frozen. Can't really speak."

"Come on," she begged. "What did they shout as they went rocketing down the slope?"

"They shouted, 'Forsooth, is not this sledding ripe with joy?'" I said.

She realized that I was making fun of her. "They didn't say that, did they, Hugh?" she asked, as hurt as a spouse had ever been.

I realized that to be withholding now was beneath my dignity as a mate. Surely I owed my wife all my powers of recollection and description. And so, I told the whole story—complete with sights, sounds, sentiment

I did it up grand—told her about Josh tumbling off the sled, rolling through the "pristine crystal snow," about Rebecca catching flakes on her tongue. I told her about the *traipsing* home—the crunching of the snow, even the clanking of the metal clips on my antique galoshes.

I embellished a little, told her a few things that never happened but would have had we stayed another few hours out in the snow.

Where was the harm? I gave my wife a gift.

Later, she gave me one back. When we were getting ready for bed, Jody came out of the bathroom wearing her cocoa apron. What happened after that is private, buddy boy. Let's just say that there is no collaboration as deep and meaningful, as co-dependent, as engaging, as ennobling as parenthood.

Daddy Has Talent

OR

Of Paternal Pluck and Drawing Ducks

Everybody knows that fatherhood reveals your limitations. But less well known is that, now and then, fatherhood also brings out skills that might well have gone undiscovered were it not for having kids. Witness the emergence of my artistic genius.

For years, I had a family reputation for being bad at drawing. In fact, Jody and the kids took great pleasure in teasing me about how bad my artwork was.

"Daddy, even David draws better than you," Rebecca once said, apparently referring to some famously ungifted kid in her class. Once we were having pizza at a local restaurant when Josh broke a silence with a nostalgic recollection. "Remember Dad's picture of the sailboat?" Rebecca laughed so hard Coke came out of her nose.

According to Jody, my drawings are not just bad, but "disturbing." She claims the neighbor's dog once got an eyeful of an O'Neill original and went whimpering out of our yard.

Don't mistake me. I earned the reputation. There is no question that for a long time I had underdeveloped spatial skills, absolutely no access to my right brain, the lobe in charge of creativity. Until that magic night.

It was 2 A.M. I couldn't sleep, so I was straightening up the living room, when I came upon one of Josh's books on the floor: *You Can Draw Animals*. Though I was pretty sure the publisher was not actually referring to me, I sat down and opened the book.

Inside were step-by-step instructions for sketching anything from a beagle to a lizard. The teaching notion was that all creatures great and small were, beneath the camouflage of fur and feathers, some combination of your basic geometric shapes. A bear's head was a sort of rounded-off triangle. An owl was a circle stacked on an oval with triangle ears.

I picked up a pencil and tried the trumpeter swan. At first I drew timidly. But then, slowly, a miracle happened. A shape vaguely reminiscent of a swan actually began to emerge. Gradually my hand moved with more confidence. It was as though somebody with a still-functional right brain had taken over my soul. By the time I used a skinny S-shaped polygon (that is, the swan's neck) to join the swan body to the swan teardrop head, I was drawing with a casual brio. I was shaping tail feathers into a swoop. I was actually cross-hatching for effect.

For the next five hours, I drew on—a man alone with his brand-new talent.

I did a chimp, a turtle, a hammerhead shark. I was Leonardo rendering muscle and form. I drew a raccoon catching a fish and a series of dog studies, one starring a litter of Dalmatian pups. The dawn found me putting the finishing touches on an opossum emerging from his burrow. When Jody came down the stairs, I showed her the opossum. She eyed me suspiciously.

"I didn't trace it. This book's amazing," I said, waving *You Can Draw Animals* in front of her. "All animals are just combos of basic shapes."

"Very good, dear," she said skeptically, heading into the kitchen to start packing lunches for school.

"You think the kids will like it?" I asked, chasing after her. "I did seventy-seven drawings."

"They'll never believe you didn't trace them," she said, slathering peanut butter.

Then Rebecca came around the corner, half-asleep, wrapped in her blue blanket.

"Look what Daddy drew," I said. She looked blearily at my masterpiece.

"Did we get more tracing paper?" she asked, turning to Jody.

"Daddy found a piece in his desk," Jody said.

"I didn't trace it! I swear!" I barked, grabbing Rebecca by her shoulders looking intensely into her eyes.

She laughed. I wept.

But despite my family's skepticism, I knew I had made a breakthrough, that I had discovered a skill that would enrich my life. If you doubt me, just compare my drawing of a jaguar before and after *You Can Draw Animals*.

Before Book

After Book

Daddy Busts His Buttons

OR

Does He?

he prophets of doom point to endless signs that our culture is in its death throes. Violence. Drugs. Divorce. Precocious sexuality. There is no shortage of apocalyptic omens. But modern-day Jeremiahs have missed the most telling sign of our demise.

Report cards.

They just ain't what they used to be. They tell parents virtually nothing about how junior is doing. They do make one thing perfectly clear: For our culture, the jig is up.

In the old days—meaning back when I was a kid— the report card was a valuable parental tool. Mom and Dad would get some vaguely objective judgment on how Annie was doing. A bunch of A's and B's meant "Better start the college fund." D's or F's, on the other hand, meant "What the hell? Might as well take that vacation now."

But today's report cards are impenetrable. They tell you nothing. Might as well be Mayan hieroglyphs. Nowhere are any of the familiar letters or numbers of yore. No A's, B's, or C's, no 83s or 95s. Instead, there is a jumble of S's and 3's and I's and 2's and NI's.

When the kids gave me their report cards last spring, I was determined to crack the code, so I consulted the legend at the top. S meant "Satisfactory," which was, believe it or not, the highest possible grade. I suddenly understood why the Japanese are clobbering our side in the trade wars. Hadn't the school board heard about searching for excellence? What if the boy Mozart had gone to the Quaker Ridge Elementary? What would he have gotten for his early compositions? S+?

I stood for "Improving," a word that by itself has no inherent meaning. Does Rebecca now think 2 + 2 = 5, instead of 6? Is Josh now able to name three of the seven continents?

NI stood for "Needs Improving." What doesn't? I thought. The Mona Lisa maybe? Tony Gwynn's batting stroke? On this report card, there was neither room for excellence nor failure. NI was the lowest possible grade, which left me to ponder how today's teacher was supposed to grade her Richie Farina, the kid in my fourth-grade class who couldn't read, write, add, and had a bad attitude to match. How was today's teacher supposed to warn Mr. and Mrs. Farina that, in her humble opinion, they should get to know a good defense attorney as soon as possible? Somehow NI lacked urgency. Were the teachers free to use S for "Sociopath"?

The absence of familiar grades was only part of the problem. The subjects themselves were strange. There were few of the old reliables. No geography. No history. No civics. Those few subjects I did recognize were divided into confounding subsections.

Mathematics, for example, included an entry called "Utilizes manipulate materials for problem-solving" which may be the only recorded use of the word "manipulate" as an adjective. At first I was delighted that Rebecca got S+, until Jody told me it only meant that our daughter knew three blocks take away one block equals two blocks.

Reading had eight subsections including "Uses knowledge of language to understand text." What else, I wondered, would you use? A spatula? Science featured "Utilizes process skills." Rebecca was apparently good at that too, though I've noticed she often seems overmatched by the "process" of making her bed.

I couldn't tell anything from their report cards. A thousand questions came to mind. Do the kids know about the bicameral legislature? Or the story of Newton getting knocked on the noggin with a Wine-sap? Can they add fractions? Do they recognize the name Paul Revere?

I know I'm a terrible old fogy—a readin'-ritin'-'rithmetic throwback to dunce-cap days. I know you're not supposed to be grade-oriented, not supposed to rank children, not supposed to put one above the other. I know you're not supposed to expect people to get the right answer as long as they use the right method. Still, I am nostalgic for the old days.

Jody says I should just relax, go with the modern flow, and take pride in the fact that our kids are straight S students. Somehow, it just doesn't do much for me.

Daddy Has a Father

OR

Of Sorrow, Zest, and All the Rest

Men like sports because they're simple. Any fool can tell who won, who lost, who got the decisive hit. Fatherhood, however, is a more subtle gig. There's no box score to tell a man how he's doing. With no clear goal line, it's tough to even tell if you're moving the ball in the right direction.

What, after all, is the Daddy mandate? To make the kids happy? Make them ready? For what? Love? Careers? Disappointment? All of the above? Some say we're supposed to give our children self-esteem. I'm not convinced. There's nothing worse than a person long on self-esteem and short on anything worth esteeming. Anyway, without a clear objective, it's easy to lose your Daddy bearings.

As always, my father is my polestar.

The original Hugh J. O'Neill was the most interesting man I've ever known. Gifted at both anger and mirth, he had the whole boatload of manly traits. All of my complicated feelings about him can be gathered into one thought: I am grateful to be his son.

In the years since his premature death, I have tried to figure out his legacy to me and to his daughters—Nancy, Kathy, Eileen, and Mary—and his other sons, Kevin and Tim.

WHEN WE WERE kids, for a month every summer my parents rented a house near the beach on Long Island. Mom and the brood would do summer in the country by the sea. Dad would work in the city during the week and drive out to Nassau Point or Shelter Island each Friday night. It was an American idyll. I remember badminton and fireflies and flippers, watermelon, waves, and wet sand. I remember fresh sheets and beds by windows. I remember tapping screens, startling moths.

Mostly I remember Dad's arrival every week.

We would all be outside in the gloaming, playing croquet or sucking on Popsicles, waiting for his trademark signal from down the road. He always honked when he crossed the causeway. His "Daddy's coming"—two shorts beeps and a long blast from the Oldsmobile—floated through the evening.

As his car pulled up, we'd all race over and greet him as though he were Elvis Presley. We'd leap on him, compete for the first hug. He'd reach out, touch, grab, tousle, kiss, yelp. In my memory, we were all, within moments, together on the beach, trying to get a kite up into the air.

Even now, I can picture my father, jacket off, tie loosened, running along the beach in wingtip shoes, trying to coax a kite into the air. We all raced along beside him as he played out the line and urged the kite skyward. "Come on, baby," he'd say as it threatened to rise—twenty, thirty, forty feet off the ground—before thwapping back to earth.

I don't think we ever got one of those kites up. This was back when kite technology was pretty crude. But Dad was tenacious, jiggling the kite cord as he ran, talking, trying to enthuse the kite up into the blue. I remember clearly those moments when the wind, for an instant, flirted with bearing the kite aloft. I remember my father's buoyant voice, full of belief that this time, at last, the kite was about to soar.

There are a thousand such moments in my memories of Dad, a thousand memories of a thousand small enthusiasms. My father had a way with joy. Though the kites didn't fly, his spirit had lift.

But this was no merely joyful man, no mere enthusiast. He also grappled with the world. He had many moments of temper, little patience for the things that intrigued ten-year-olds. He was a doctor and so lived in the brutal world of test results and waiting rooms. He heard the lamentation as well as the laughter.

I can remember, as a teenager, watching him from afar. His face was a storm of thoughtfulness, a field of worry and concern. His eyes mourned and flashed. Even to a sunny kid, it was clear that he was wrestling with big thoughts: the tragedy in the Kelly family, the shiver of things he had seen at war, questions about how to serve his God and sustain his family. My father had a man's secrets. He had gravity about him. To him, the world was serious, engaging, and full of delight and woe. From Hugh J. O'Neill there came a pulse that felt, to his son, like a promise. There would be much to learn in this life. There would be stories to hear. Life would offer a guy all he could handle.

My father sang the whole song. Whenever I think of him, I summon a man with access to all of life's humors, a man who knew that life was neither a cabaret nor a catastrophe. It was both.

Maybe the goal of fatherhood can be no more specific than this: to commend our children out into the world with full minds, undiminished by cynicism, unsullied by our stupidities, susceptible to all the world's sounds, to its high notes and the low notes, to both its unexplained elations and uninvited sorrows.

How to do that? I haven't a clue. But just having a goal may help you move the ball down the field.

How Does Daddy Love Thee?

OR

The Poetry of Poppa

The idea of fatherhood made him feel poetical and proud," E. B. White wrote in *The Trumpet of the Swan*. Though the father in White's novel is a bird, the sentiment cuts across species. Tending children inclines a man to big, even poetic, feelings.

I ARRIVED AT Josh's room and clicked the Mets postgame show off his radio. As I closed the window against the night, he turned over in his sleep, flopping that face into the moonlight. It was, even in repose, full of moves. A wrinkle of woe, a sliver of smile. The boy was a sweaty engine—idling away under the covers—storing up juice for tomorrow.

When the small scar on his upper lip quivered, I remembered his Christmas Eve courage in the emergency room. I knew that I was flirting with yet another flood of father feeling, that I should get out of that room before I lost it. But I didn't leave. Instead, I sat down on the edge of his bed, ran my hand over his crewcut, and tumbled, once more out of control, into a familiar fatherhood cascade.

I remembered it all—the apple-juice flood, the second-grade drum solo, the pudding on the piano keys. I flashed through a thousand and one nights of euphoria and fatigue. I remembered watermelon juice darting down chins in late-summer light, mosquitoes wheering in our ears. I remembered cookies and crayons and the month Rebecca spoke with a cockney accent.

And then, listening to Josh's little night sounds—murmur, slurp, and click—I remembered the time *before* I had the kids and their ascent to life awakened my attention. I remembered the quiet time before the reveille of these two.

Since I have been a father, the pendulum of my life swings through a wider arc. Before Josh and Rebecca, I rarely whispered and I rarely yelled. Now I do both all the time. Before Josh and Rebecca, I merely strode through the world like a man. Now I crawl, hunker, scramble, hop on one foot, often see the world from my hands and knees. Before Josh and Rebecca, I knew nothing about waterslides. Now I hold several American records in the over-thirty-five division. Before Josh and Rebecca, I heard only the sound of my own voice. Now I sometimes hear the principal, asking to see me at my "earliest possible convenience." Now I always carry two small voices in my soul. Before Josh and Rebecca, the world was plain. Now it's fancy, full of portents and omens, comic books and ant farms, solemnity and awe.

Sitting next to Josh in the half-light, I felt, at last, a link between the passions of my heart and the work of my days. I felt enriched by my past, bound to the future, and embedded in right now. I felt susceptible to everything—the high notes, the low notes, all of it.

E. B. White was wrong about pride coming with fatherhood. In fact, fatherhood is as humbling as it gets. But he was right about the poetry of poppa. Like the poet, Daddy traffics in frozen moments. And like the poet, his senses are quickened. Daddy is forever on the verge of either alas or hallelujah. Poetry and paternity are of imagination compact. Both the cadence of verse and the ragged rhythms of family life endorse the beating of our hearts.

Josh's eyes fluttered open. "Dad," he said sleepily, not at all surprised to find me looming over him yet again. "The Mets won in the bottom of the ninth."

"Great, that's great," I managed to get out. As he closed his eyes and drifted back to sleep, from down the hall, my daughter cried out in her sleep. Sitting there, in the sweet wreckage of my boy's room, amid all the baseball cards and hope, I could feel the rising of the wind.

The Ten Commandments of Daddy

OR

At Last, Some Rules to Live By

I have found the fundamental laws of father-hood. The skeptics said it couldn't be done. Fatherhood is too complicated, they cried, to be reduced to capsule form. But complexity only added intrigue to the quest for guiding principles.

After all the emotions, all the yelling, and all the laughter, I have actually distilled the duties and demands down to a decade of Daddy dicta. Herewith, on behalf of all God's children and their male parents, the Ten Commandments of Daddy.

I
Hey, Dad, Be Big

Figuratively, that is. Fatherhood is still a star turn. Granted, some of that patriarchal stuff is withering. But you're still the strongest guy in the house. That counts. Consider some of the guys who have gone before you: *Father* Time, the Founding *Fathers*, God the

Father. It's a powerful tradition. The kids expect some stature from you. You can't give this role a walk-through. Got to play it.

Now this doesn't mean you can choose any old vivid persona. After all, Genghis Khan was plenty vivid, and his kids didn't have an easy time. But you can't be a blank slate. The kids ought to know what the old man would think about this or that. You are the anvil on which they hammer out their deal with the world. Be a presence in their lives—and minds.

II
Hey, Dad, Be Small

Yes, this directly contradicts the first commandment. I told you, fatherhood is complicated.

Don't be so big that you suck all the air out of the room. Give your kids a little space to move around in, to test their thoughts and strengths. Take a back seat, figuratively speaking, three, four times a week. Say, "Maybe." Say, "I don't know." Now and then, tell the kids you're sorry. Plenty of things to apologize for: anger, inattention, bad career planning, lack of whatever. Mean it. Be sorry. You'll feel brand-new.

III
Hey, Dad, Come Home

To be sure, the obligations of making a living can keep you out of the house. Lots of fathers have a day job and a night job. If that's your situation, God bless you, pal. You'll get no heat from me. But if you can pay the bills without working double-shift, you've got to be home when you can. You don't have to be playing catch all the time or even talking to the kids. But at least, be present. Get off the golf course. Head home. Nothing good can happen until you do.

IV
Honor Thy Father and Mother

This actually is the biblical Fourth Commandment. It's included here only because now that I am one of the guys getting the honoring, I like the sound of it much more than I did when I was a boy.

V
Bob and Weave, Dad, Bob and Weave

Stay light on your feet, Dad. Don't make too many hard-and-fast rules. Don't draw too many lines in the sand. This doesn't mean anything goes; there are rules. It just means that fatherhood is an improvisation and that human hearts—both yours and the children's—have a way with compromise. Don't insist on having your way with the kids just because the rest of the world isn't always overly interested in the sound of your voice. There is a difference between authority and power. Have the first; don't abuse the second.

VI
Thou Shalt Not Dance in Front of Your Kids' Friends

My own father once picked us up at a junior high school dance. As usual, he was wearing his wingtip shoes and that hat he got through the mail from Ireland. As we were walking out of the gym, he actually did a few seconds of the hully-gully with a horrified Margie Costanzo. My sister Kathy still has nightmares about it.

If you've got to dance, dance with Mom in private. Don't embarrass everybody with your version of the Hustle.

VII
Save Your Money, Big Man

You know all those corny proverbs about pennies saved. If you're not careful, the kids will send you to the poorhouse a dollar and nineteen cents at a time. Think college tuition. Think down payment on their starter homes. Though it's true that money can't buy happiness, it can buy lots of other stuff. Believe in compound interest, tax-free growth. For God's sake, champ, be ready for emergencies.

VIII
Spend Your Money, Tightwad

You see what I'm after here, don't you? F. Scott Fitzgerald said the sign of a first-rate mind was the ability to have two opposite opinions at the same time. Never mind that he fell victim to drink. You're a first-rate mind, Dad.

Spring for the glowing monster trading cards. If you've got the money, pop for that musical princess crown. What are you saving the money for, pal? College? Hah! You can't save enough anyway. There is the future and then there is now. This is not a dress rehearsal. This is it.

IX
Never Go on an Amusement Park Ride with the Word "Whirl" in Its Name, Especially the Space Shuttle Whirl at Great Escape Near Lake George, New York

Even though you want to participate with the kids, to feel their gravity-defying thrill/terror/glee, you mustn't get on that ride with them. I did in the summer of 1993 and have been a little queasy ever since. It's tough to be a good father when your central nervous system is on the fritz. Stay on the ground and wave.

X
This Is Their Life, Not a Second Chance at Yours

I can't say it any better than one of the most eminent psychiatrists of our time, Bruno Bettelheim: "We

221

become upset when we believe we see in a child aspects of our own personalities of which we disapprove." On the money. It's tempting to make good on your own shortcomings through your children. Just because you didn't make the varsity at North Salem High doesn't mean Stan Jr. has to. Help them follow *their* path, not your road-not-taken.

Xa
Love Their Mother

One extra commandment—to grow on. Hug Mom. Often. In front of the kids. Be grateful to her. Speak to her with respect. Try to make her laugh. Listen.

WHEN ALL IS said and done, fatherhood comes down to this. Be big. Be small. Be quiet. Make noise. Don't dance in front of your kids' friends. Save. Spend. Stay off the whirling ride of death. And love their mother.

And one more thing. You remember that plastic sword? The one I carried up the stairs The Night of the Great Fall? The weapon I adopted as a symbol of Daddy courage? Well, even a *plastic* sword has too much swagger to stand for Daddy strength.

"The weapons with which we have gained our most important victories," wrote Thoreau, "which should be handed down from father to son, are not the sword and the lance, but the bushwhack, the turf-cutter, the spade and the bog-hoe." The triumphs of Dad are about tenacity, keeping on.

So do whatever it takes. Stay loose. Use all the clubs in the bag. Hit the ball to all fields. Use whatever sports metaphor works for you. Just be sure to use your body, your voice, your memory, everything you've got. Whisper. Shout. Encourage. Goad. Cultivate the garden. Forgive. Be patient. Watch closely. Enjoy.